FAST to the TABLE
FREEZER COOKBOOK

Freezer-Friendly Recipes and Frozen Food Shortcuts

Fast to the TABLE
FREEZER COOKBOOK

Freezer-Friendly Recipes and Frozen Food Shortcuts

Becky Rosenthal

The Countryman Press
A division of W. W. Norton & Company
Independent Publishers Since 1923

To my husband, who eats and loves everything I create; and to Everett, our sweet son and budding foodie who, though he loves a good meal, would rather a *quickly* prepared meal, and thus has enjoyed my new practice of freezing.

For information about permission to reproduce selections from this book, write to Permissions, The Countryman Press, 500 Fifth Avenue, New York, NY 10110

For information about special discounts for bulk purchases, please contact W. W. Norton Special Sales at specialsales@wwnorton.com or 800-233-4830

Manufacturing by Quad/Graphics, Taunton
Book design by LeAnna Weller Smith

The Countryman Press
www.countrymanpress.com

A division of W. W. Norton & Company, Inc.
500 Fifth Avenue, New York, NY 10110
www.wwnorton.com

978-1-58157-382-4

Food is best when shared and even better when thoughtfully prepared in advance.

CONTENTS

INTRODUCTION

I have dreamed of a world in which I can bring dinner to a sick friend while simultaneously having a hot meal prepared for my family, fresh cookies in the oven, and the option of feeding anyone who happens to drop by at any time. Somehow this never seems to work. I have, however, discovered a secret to getting closer to making this dream a reality . . . FREEZING MEALS AHEAD OF TIME AND USING FROZEN FOODS TO COOK!

Now, when I make a dish for my family, I double it so that half goes straight to the freezer for either a busy weeknight meal or to take to a friend. The same goes for when I'm making muffins, quiche, soup, and pizza. If I have extra soup, I'll pour it into a pint jar and freeze that for a lunch or sick day. Play dates turn into cooking dates with friends so both our kids and the moms have some fun. And free afternoons are taken advantage of with bigger projects such as homemade gnocchi, salted caramel brownies, chicken or beef stock, or sauces—all to make weeknight meals easier, all with which to stock the freezer, all because . . . I do still love to cook.

I have also started freezing fresh foods, especially fruits and vegetables when they are at their peak ripeness. If you're a person who shops at a big box store or farmers' markets, but finds yourself overwhelmed by the quantities in which the food is sold, you can break down nearly everything to freeze in more reasonable quantities. For example, beef or chicken. You can either cook the meat first and use it in a recipe for enchiladas or pasta—this makes for the quickest cooking once you're ready—or freeze the cooked meat for future recipes in smaller containers. I have also found making homemade stocks and sauces to be easy and helpful for assembling a quick meal. My recipes use these frozen components to make great dishes.

I used to think people who ate freezer meals were willing to sacrifice taste for convenience. But it can be quite the opposite. I love cooking and sharing food with friends so much that I've discovered the freezer is the best way to help me accomplish both of these pleasures. Plus, when I use my freezer to store up different components of a recipe, my food ends up tasting even better. My friend Adam opened my eyes to this.

He runs his own catering business all by himself and it thrives because he always utilizes his freezer in order to be efficient with his time and to not waste food. If he has extra-ripe bananas, he freezes them mashed up so they're ready for banana bread pudding, and if he makes a large batch of soup or sauce he makes sure to pack some away for future gigs.

While writing this book, I actually did host several parties on the fly. I've delivered countless meals to friends and even people I barely know. I now prep for the holidays in early November, making a big batch of Honey Nut Sticky Buns or quiche so that on the mornings of Thanksgiving and Christmas, all I have to do is bake the dishes for a special breakfast. Food, friends, and family are all enjoyed without having to sacrifice any of them.

Just so you know, I also have this obsession with fresh foods. I am a member of a local CSA, so we get farm-fresh produce weekly. We eat seasonally and believe that fresh is best. While in the past I've enjoyed canning to preserve some of this fresh food, I have now found that freezing to preserve is just as effective and much easier. I now make freezer jam instead of canning it and I don't have to worry about pectin, sugar content, or proper sealing in a water bath. In the late summer, I freeze peach halves to enjoy when we need a little taste of sunshine midwinter, and we always block out an afternoon to make homemade tomato sauce that we can savor throughout the cold season.

Things weren't always sunny at our house. Before making this book, I cooked almost every night and when we brought dinner to friends it usually (or almost always) took a toll on my entire family. Just a few months ago, my freezer was literally broken, leaking on one end, with questionable fruit and veggies in partially opened bags, unlabeled frozen meat, and a few unknown leftovers inside. It was constantly defrosting, giving my toddler a small puddle-jumping pond to splash in. The food inside went from frozen to melted and back to frozen again. There was only one good side to all of this . . . perfectly melted ice cream, that point when the ice cream is at just the right cold and creamy temperature.

Well, when I took on this book, I knew I would have to find another way to get my ice cream the perfect consistency because this freezer had to work! Not only had I signed the contract for this book, we were approaching the best harvest of summer and I knew I wanted to save all of the best produce of the year such as that sweet yellow corn and those bright green peas I spotted filling a truck bed at the market.

Luckily, we fixed the freezer just in time to save summer.

In this book, you'll find lots of fresh ideas to use for your freezer—not just casseroles and bagged frozen foods from the grocery store, but foods that hold onto the flavors of a different season, saving time as you make dinner quicker and more efficiently. And yes, we'll cover ice cream too—really, really good ice cream. You can start with stocks and sauces, building a base for future recipes in your freezer, or you can jump right into the recipes, choosing whichever ones sound good to you.

I will tell you that freezing foods, much like eating them, is best when done with others. Grab a few friends and lots of fresh corn and get to work shucking, or make several dishes of enchiladas to deliver to new parents. You'll have bags of corn and platters of enchiladas ready in no time, all done in good company.

A friend recently mailed me a couple of her grandmother's vintage cookbooks. One, titled

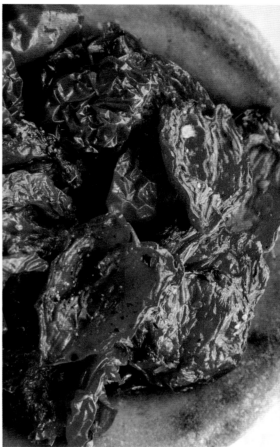

The Enterprising Housekeeper and published in 1898, asked some surprisingly timely questions: "The demand at the present time is not so much to do with new directions for old methods, as for the suggestions and recipes relating especially to the use of time saving 'left-overs.' What to do with food left from the previous meal? How may I use this that my table may be set economically and well? How can I vary the recipes that these left-overs may appear in appetizing and tempting forms for several succeeding meals?" For centuries, home cooks have been trying to not be wasteful, saving time and money in the kitchen. It's beautiful how these questions are as relevant today as they were in the late 19th century.

My hope is that by using your freezer more, and more effectively, you'll be able to share your food, save time and money, and not let anything go to waste. My other hope is that this book can inspire others in the same stage of life as me, as well as those who are not, to get back into the joy of cooking.

Now, pour yourself a glass of wine or a cup of coffee, whatever your pleasure, and let's get started. We have a freezer to fill!

FREEZING BASICS

As my dad might say, "Freezing is not rocket science." As a once rocket scientist, he's allowed to say that, I guess, but in this case it's really true. If you prefer the simplest form of preserving food, freezing just may be your match. Freezing is also the least time-consuming way to preserve food. Once you start practicing freezing foods, you'll easily get the hang of it and this section of the book will seem like common sense. Before you begin the process, however, it is good to learn the best practices behind freezing to maintain the quality of the food you freeze.

The basic steps to ensure best results when freezing:

- Prepare your food quickly.
- Package your food in moisture- and vapor-proof wrapping or containers—products that don't permit the introduction of air or moisture.
- Use the correct packaging and freezing method for the specific food you're freezing.
- Keep your freezer at 0°F or cooler.
- Properly thaw your food to preserve its quality and prevent bacterial growth.

Getting the Freezer Ready

To get a good freezing system in place, you really don't need much. In fact, most of what you do need, you probably already have around your kitchen.

First and foremost, you will need a working freezer. This may sound silly but as I started this book, my own freezer was not in perfect working order. Your freezer needs to be set at a steady temperature of 0°F or lower and be free of any ice crystals or frost. You might even want to purchase a freezer thermometer to monitor the internal temperature of your freezer. Make sure to go through what you currently have in your freezer and toss out what might be out of date, questionable, or unknown. I will be the first to admit that I throw bags or jars of things in my freezer, thinking I will remember what they are, only later to have no idea what the frozen substance is.

You may also want to look into getting a chest freezer; that is, if you're really gearing up to freeze food regularly. When I began writing this book, I invested in a chest freezer and four months later, both my regular freezer and chest freezer were full. So, not a problem to have an extra freezer, especially if you're about to head into winter!

Basic Freezing Supplies

Next, you'll need to check your supplies. My most commonly used freezing supplies are parchment paper, plastic wrap, baking sheets, large bowls, foil, freezer-safe packaging (we'll get to that in a second), and a felt-tip marker for labeling. These are worth buying in bulk if you have high hopes of stocking your freezer. Other supplies are not necessary but definitely useful, such as a vacuum sealer, a hands-free rack for pouring soups and so on into bags, ice cube trays (regular or silicone), standard muffin tins or silicone muffin pans, and freezer-safe glass jars.

The best and most common types of packaging are freezer-safe resealable plastic bags, disposable foil containers, vacuum-seal bags, rigid plastic containers, and glass jars. Here is a brief description of each and how best to use them:

Freezer safe-resealable plastic bags: Make sure to check the labels when you buy plastic bags, to ensure that they are freezer safe and that they press or zip shut securely rather than need to be tied. Also, force out any excess air before sealing and storing.

Disposable foil containers: These are great for casseroles, baked breads, and frozen pizza. When using these, make sure to wrap the food tightly in plastic wrap, then foil, and to label the top of the packaging. I especially like using these when I bring food to friends and don't want them to have the hassle of getting my dish back to me or if I don't want one of my baking dishes occupied in the freezer. The sizes I like to have around are 9 x 13-inch rectangular pans, 9-inch square pans, 9 x 5-inch loaf pans, 9-inch pie plates, and pizza pans.

Vacuum-seal bags: The vacuum-sealing process is recommended for cooked or raw meats. I also use it for some vegetables, such as corn or shredded zucchini, as well as cooked and drained beans and slow-roasted tomatoes. This packaging ensures that the food doesn't get freezer burn, and in turn, lengthens its freezer life.

Rigid plastic containers: These are suitable for soft or liquid foods, such as soups, stews, and stocks. Freezer-safe plastic snap-top containers may be used, as well as freezer-safe plastic jars. Make sure to check the label of the product before using.

Glass jars: Only use canning jars with straight edges and make sure to not fill them up to the top, allowing room for the liquid to expand.

Following are a few basic ways to freeze. The recipes in this book refer back to these, so that you know which method to use with each food item.

Freezing Methods
LAY OUT AND FREEZE METHOD

For this method, you simply lay out the food (say, fruit or gnocchi) in a single layer, not overlapping, on a parchment-lined baking sheet. Place the baking sheet on a level shelf in the freezer and let freeze overnight, or until frozen solid (the time depends on the weight and density of the food). Once the food item is frozen, you can transfer it to a freezer-safe resealable plastic bag to store in the freezer. Make sure your bag is labeled with the food item and date.

I like to portion out foods into smaller quantities that make sense for my family. For example, I might divide frozen gnocchi into 2-cup portions and place them in quart-size bags. If you're freezing fruit, you might want to divide the fruit into smaller, separate packs for smoothies, so that you don't need to take all the fruit out of the freezer every time you make a smoothie.

DIVIDE AND PORTION METHOD

This method is best when you make anything that is liquid, such as soup, stews, sauces, and vegetables, and it's also the method used for cooked or raw meats, vegetables, and beans.

In plastic bags: For this you'll want to have ready freezer-safe resealable plastic bags. Divide the item into portions that make sense for your family. For our family of three I like to use gallon-size bags and fill them with 5 to 6 cups of soup or stew to yield three dinner-size portions. For a lunch portion for two people, I would freeze about 3 cups in a quart-size bag. Once you have divided your food among the bags, make sure you press all the air out of the bags and seal them completely.

To freeze, lay the bag flat in the freezer. You can lay the bag between two sheet pans or just on something that seems evenly flat. Once the bag is frozen, you can store it standing upright to save space. My friend Anne does this and her freezer looks like a filing system. She also places the label at the top of the bags so that she can read what they contain without pulling the bags out. Have a space in your freezer dedicated to filing or stacking frozen sauces and soups using this method.

Vacuum-sealing: For some specific foods I like to use a vacuum-seal bag system, using the same procedure as the Plastic Bag Method to freeze them, but just getting a really airtight seal. Cooked meats, corn, zucchini, beans, and bacon are all ones I would recommend using a vacuum sealer for (if you have one).

In rigid plastic containers: For stocks and larger quantities of sauces I like to use rigid plastic containers instead of bags. I use quart-size freezer-safe plastic containers. I usually thaw 1 quart for a soup recipe, or two if it's a bigger portion of soup.

In jars: Check the label of the jar package to make sure it has a freezer-safe designation on it. Most straight-sided jars, such as canning jars, are freezer safe. Also, make sure to not fill the jars completely. Leave at least 1/2 inch of headspace for the expansion of the liquid in the freezer. I like to put away a few soups in jars for lunches and sick-day gifts. I also use jars for jam, ice cream with cake, and some sauces. Jars definitely take up more freezer space than bags, but it's fun to have a jar of cake and ice cream ready to give away to a friend.

CASSEROLE METHOD

You want to let the food item cool if it has been already baked, then wrap it tightly with plastic wrap, below and all around the dish. The tight layer of plastic wrap is to prevent any moisture, which could lead to freezer burn and flavor loss. Then cover it all again with foil. On top of the foil, label the item along with any baking instructions and a reminder to remove the plastic before cooking (leaving it on is a messy mistake to make). This method is best for lasagna, baked French toast, quiche, pumpkin bread, and really anything that is stored in a disposable foil container, such as the Lemon Cream Bars (page 184) and Honey Nut Sticky Buns (page 59).

PIZZA METHOD

Build your pizza on a disposable pizza pan and wrap tightly and all around with plastic wrap and then foil. Label, then freeze. Remove the plastic wrap and foil before baking. Bake for 2 minutes longer than if baking fresh.

WRAP AND BAG METHOD

For smaller handheld foods, such as burritos, hand pies, brownies on a stick, and so on, you'll want to wrap them individually and tightly in plastic wrap, then place them in a larger, freezer-safe resealable plastic bag. Occasionally, I'll freeze an item first, using the Lay Out and Freeze Method (see page 14), before wrapping it, but overall the simplest way is to wrap, then bag, and into the freezer it goes. Doughs, such as the Pizza Dough (page 215) and Pie Dough (page 167), are also frozen this way.

ICE CUBE METHOD

This method is useful for sauces and stocks. When I make a big portion of chicken stock, I usually freeze some by this method, so that I have some in smaller portions, as well as some packaged in quart-size containers.

For this method you'll pour or spoon out the food item into small portions, then freeze. Once they are frozen, you can transfer the individual portions to a larger freezer-safe plastic bag. You don't only have to use ice cube trays; you can also use muffin tins. Silicone ice cube trays or muffin pans make removing the frozen items easy, they come in several different sizes and shapes suitable for freezing small portions. That said, I still freeze my pesto the classic way in an ice cube tray. For applesauce, I like to use a muffin tin so that my son has the prefect portion for a snack.

To remove the food from a standard muffin tin (not silicone) place the frozen tray over a larger rimmed baking sheet filled with warm water. Once the food (such as applesauce) starts to loosen around the edges, you can remove the disks and place them in a larger freezer-safe resealable plastic bag. If the food thaws a little too much, you may want to refreeze the disks on their parchment until they are completely solid again before placing in the bag, so they don't stick together.

Common Topics in Freezing

Thawing: Make sure to use correct thawing measures for each specific food. Thawing in your refrigerator is the safest and best way to thaw food. This takes a little planning, but is well worth it. Other methods including placing a bag of frozen food into cold water (never hot or warm water), or microwaving on a DEFROST setting. Thaw only what you need and use your food immediately upon thawing. If your thawed food smells or tastes odd, don't hesitate to dispose of it.

Refreezing: Refreezing food is not recommend as a regular practice, but if you take out some food from the freezer in hopes of using it but don't quite get to it, as long as it still has some ice crystals on it, it may be refrozen. You should know that its quality of taste and texture may be compromised. If certain foods, such as vegetables and meats (low-acidic foods) have been completely defrosted, they shouldn't be refrozen. You may refreeze fruit or high-acidic foods if they are still cold. Refrozen foods last a shorter amount of time in the freezer than when they were first frozen.

Freezer burn: Freezer burn is the result of air's coming into contact with your food. Sometimes this produces a change of color, texture, or flavor. The air removes moisture and causes the food to dry out. This may occur due to improper wrapping, incorrect storage, or an unsuitable freezer container.

Labeling: Before filling it, label each package with the item name and date it was made. You may also want to note the quantity/servings and reheating/thawing instructions. In addition to labeling your frozen food, you may want to keep a written record of what's in your freezer and its expiration. This may be logged in a small notebook or onto a whiteboard attached to your freezer.

Organizing your freezer: It's easy when you start to get into freezing for your freezer to get out of control and unorganized. Start with a good system and try to keep it (talking to myself, too, here!). I like to keep all my veggie bags in one large plastic grocery sack of a specific color (green) and same with all of my frozen fruits. If all your bagged fruit is in one larger bag, then you won't have to dig through the freezer looking for the right fruit. Same goes with meats, keeping frozen and raw in separate bags.

Try to organize in such a way that the things you use most often are at the top (smoothie packs, ice cubed sauces, frozen burritos, falafel), and the items you use less often at the bottom, such as large containers of stock, beef or chicken bones, and so on. It's also good to specify an area for larger casserole dishes, such as enchiladas, pasta bakes, quiches, and so on. I stand all my bagged sauces and soups upright in a filing system, and keep my stocks in plastic containers at the bottom of the freezer.

If you have a chest freezer that comes with a rack on top and you can find a second rack, it's convenient to have two, so you have more space for those items you want to have accessible. Then, you can tie your larger bags of fruits and vegetables to the bottom of the rack.

What NOT to freeze: cakes with frosting, custards or cream pie fillings, egg whites or meringues, mayonnaise, raw fruits and vegetables with high water content, gravy, yogurt, cream cheese, and sour cream.

HOW TO FREEZE FOOD

Fruit

Preserving fresh fruit by freezing requires hardly any preparation and takes about one third of the time that canning does—and it doesn't require any sugar. The key to great frozen fruit starts with perfectly ripe fruit. Don't feel that you have to grow your own fruits to reap these benefits; just wait until your favorite fruits are in season and buy them from a local farmers' market. Here are the simple steps I use to freeze fruit along with a few specific examples:

1. Choose perfectly ripe fruit.
2. Freeze in small, manageable quantities (1 to 2 quarts at a time).
3. Wash your fruit, then lay it out to dry before freezing it.
4. Use the Lay Out and Freeze Method (see page 14) to freeze and store.
5. Try not to set out the whole bag of frozen fruit on the counter every time you make a recipe with frozen fruit, smoothies, and so on, so that the fruit doesn't get ice crystals. (Packing frozen fruit into several smaller bags may help with this.)
6. Use frozen fruit within 1 year.

What not to freeze: Really juicy fruit, such as melon, doesn't freeze well, though you can freeze watermelon juice in ice cubes for fruited water, cocktails, or smoothies.

AVOCADOS

When avocados are on sale or if you just happen to have too many ripe avocados on hand, purée them all, then divide the purée by the cupful into pint-size freezer-safe resealable plastic bags. While frozen avocado is not best for guacamole, it does make a great base for sauces, such as Avocado Crema (page 74) or salad dressings.

BERRIES

Rinse the berries gently, getting rid of any leaves, stems, dirt, and so on. Lay them out flat on a paper towel to dry. Snag a few for a working snack (preserving food has its rewards). Once dry, transfer the berries to a large, parchment-lined baking sheet (a half sheet pan). Make sure the fruit isn't overlapping. Let freeze overnight or for several hours until frozen solid. Once frozen, use a spatula to scrape the berries off the parchment, if necessary, and transfer to a gallon-size, labeled, freezer-safe resealable plastic bag, or divide out for smoothie packs.

Note: If the berries break up a little, it's okay; just freeze all of them, even if they are a little mushy or broken (the tiny berries are especially delicate and delicious).

STONE FRUIT

You can freeze stone fruit peeled or unpeeled. In either case, rinse the fruit, then slice into desired size wedges or in half. Remove the pits. Toss with freshly squeezed lemon juice, then freeze on a parchment-lined sheet pan, arranged in a single layer, cut side up. The lemon juice will help the fruit retain its color.

A farmer once told me that the best way to freeze peaches is just to peel, then slice in half and freeze. He stores them in a grocery bag (the

plastic kind with handles) so that he can easily reach in and grab one without pulling the whole bag out and causing some to unfreeze. While the peaches are a perfect snack as is, they are even better with a little yogurt and granola (see page 84) on top. Or if you need a quick dessert, place a scoop of Vanilla Ice Cream (page 168) in the center of each peach half.

How to peel peaches before freezing: This method is best done with fully ripe peaches. To peel the peaches, bring a large pot of water to a boil. Prepare a large bowl of ice water. Use a paring knife to score an X on the bottom of every peach, being careful to not slice too deeply, or else the peach will cook through (which you don't want). Carefully place the peaches in the boiling water for 30 seconds to 2 minutes (depending on the ripeness of the peach). The peach is ready when the skin stars to peel away at the X. Use a slotted spoon to transfer the peaches to the ice water. Let them cool for just a minute or two, then transfer them to a large surface to start peeling. Refill the bowl with fresh ice water plus ½ lemon with its juices and rind (to prevent the peaches from oxidizing and changing color) and place the peeled peaches into the lemon ice water as you work on peeling the rest. After they are all peeled, slice, then set them out to dry on a wire rack before freezing.

BANANAS

A wise mom once told me that she saves ends of the bananas that her kids didn't finish. She would slice off the bit portion and freeze the ends of those banana pieces and use them in smoothies. Although my kiddo has never left even a small bite of a banana behind, I took the tip and mentally stored it away. Now I just buy extra bananas when they are cheap, slice them, and use the Lay Out and Freeze Method (see page 14) to freeze them. Or if you have brown bananas on your counter but don't have the time to make banana bread or banana waffles, mash them, then freeze the mash in a freezer-safe resealable plastic bag. I like to freeze mashed bananas in two-banana portions, which is about what normal banana bread or my Banana Waffles recipe (page 49) calls for.

GRAPES

Rinse the grapes, then lay out to dry on a kitchen towel. Once dry, remove the grapes from their stems, then use the Lay Out and Freeze Method (see page 14) to freeze.

Vegetables

At the end of the summer this year I stocked up on cheap farmers' market fresh veggies. Here are my tips for freezing veggies:

- Make a plan of what veggies you want to freeze.
- Check the Frozen Vegetable Chart (page 25) to see whether you should blanch a particular vegetable before freezing it.
- Prepare your veggies (slice, julienne, etc.) in bite-size pieces according to how they will be used (see the Frozen Vegetable Chart).
- Freeze the sliced veggies, using the Lay Out and Freeze Method (see page 14), when appropriate. For grated and mashed vegetables, simply freeze in a freezer-safe resealable plastic bag. For convenient storage, press the bag flat before freezing.
- Portion frozen veggies into the bags in quantities appropriate for your family.
- Combine in the same bag veggies that go

well together in several dishes or as a side dish. My friend Madelyn and I came up with three types of veggie bags that we knew we would use up over the winter, and one afternoon we prepped and bagged several big bags of veggies. From these I make my Thai Noodles with Veggies and Peanut Sauce (page 157) and Orange Sesame Beef Stir-Fry (page 133), and I complement so many meals with simple steamed prefrozen veggies.

THREE FREEZER BAG IDEAS

Asian
For stir-fries or Thai peanut noodles:

peppers

carrots, julienned

snow peas

green beans

broccoli, cut into florets

Classic
For steaming, stir-fries, or with tomato sauce or pesto:

broccoli, cut into florets

carrots, sliced

cauliflower, cut into florets

green beans

Fajitas
For bean and rice bowls, fajitas, or as a side to any Mexican dish, such as enchiladas:

onions, chopped or sliced

green and red bell peppers, seeded and chopped or sliced

CORN

Freezing fresh, midsummer corn was one of the first freezer projects I took on. It's a great one to accomplish with a friend or two. When corn is at the height of its season, it's not only sweeter; it's much cheaper as well. Freezing corn is quite simple. Here's how I like to do it:

Take the husks off the cobs and rinse all the corn, getting rid of any strings, dirt, or friendly worms (you can cut off any parts of ears that have been enjoyed by these critters). Bring a large pot of water to a boil and blanch the corn for 3 to 4 minutes. Remove the cobs and place them in a bowl of ice water just for a minute or two. Then, you will need two bowls: one small and one as large as you have. Place the small bowl upside down inside the larger one. This becomes a little pedestal to put your cob on while you shave the corn off the ear. Use a sharp knife to slice the corn away from the ear and into the larger bowl. Repeat with the remaining cobs. Lay out the corn on a parchment-lined baking sheet to dry slightly. Divide the corn into labeled freezer-safe resealable plastic bags or vacuum-sealed bags (I prefer the latter for corn). Two cups is a good amount per bag. Place in the freezer.

Don't throw away the corncobs, they make a great corn stock for Smoky Corn and Bacon Chowder (page 98)!

FROZEN VEGETABLE CHART

The vegetables listed here can all be stored in freezer-safe resealable plastic bags.

VEGETABLE	SIZE	BLANCHING TIME
Asparagus	Half-inch pieces	2 minutes
Bell peppers	Stemmed and seeded; slice into uniform strips	none
Broccoli	Half-inch pieces, sliced	3 to 4 minutes
Brussels sprouts	Stemmed; keep whole or slice in half	3 to 5 minutes
Carrots	Peeled, then sliced	2 minutes
Cauliflower	Half-inch pieces, broken	3 minutes, in 1 tablespoon vinegar to 1 gallon water
Corn	Whole ears; cut kernels after blanching and cooling	4 minutes
Green beans	Whole or sliced into 1-inch pieces	2 to 4 minutes
Greens (spinach or chard)	Washed, thick stems removed	1½ minutes, stirring constantly
Onions	Sliced into strips or chopped	none
Snow peas	whole	1½ minutes
Winter squash	Peeled and seeded, cut into half-inch cubes	none, or cook, then mash or purée
Zucchini/summer squash	Grated or shredded	2 minutes

Thawing vegetables: Most frozen vegetables hold up best when cooked without thawing first. You can steam, boil, microwave, or sauté frozen vegetables. Expect a little excess water in your recipes when using frozen vegetables. Frozen greens, such as spinach, are best partially thawed, squeezing out any excess water, before using.

Pumpkin

Makes the equivalent of 2 (16-ounce) cans purée

This year I started decorating with pie pumpkins (the smaller variety that are best for making pumpkin purée) instead of large ones. This way, once the harvest decorating season is over, I can bake my cute decorations. I use the purée for pancakes and waffles, oatmeal, bread, pies, and just about anything I can think of to give a pumpkin flavor. And you'll quickly realize that homemade pumpkin purée is well worth the little bit of extra effort.

2 pie pumpkins (a little less than 2 pounds each)   **Water**

1. Preheat the oven to 400°F and get out a large, rimmed baking sheet.

2. Slice the pumpkins in half and remove their seeds and stringy insides (if you happen to have a pumpkin-carving tool kit, the orange scoop is really useful for this!).

3. Place the pumpkins, cut side down, on the baking sheet. Place the baking sheet in the oven, then use a large liquid measuring cup to pour water into the pan, to about ¼ inch deep. (This is easier than pouring the water in the pan and then trying to bring the pan across your kitchen to place it in the oven.) Make sure the water also gets beneath the pumpkin halves.

4. Roast the pumpkin for 40 minutes. You're really steaming the pumpkin with the water, which will create a really moist purée.

5. Remove the pan carefully from the oven (the water is very hot at this point) and pour off the water into the sink. Let the pumpkins rest and cool (the pumpkin will deflate like a balloon—this is okay).

5. Once cool, use a large spoon or a pumpkin scoop to scoop the flesh of the pumpkin from the skin. Toss out the skin and purée the pumpkin in a food processor or blender. Refrigerate if using within a week, or freeze.

TO FREEZE: Spoon the purée into quart-size freezer-safe resealable plastic bags in 15-ounce proportions or in proportions right for your favorite pumpkin recipes (the standard can size for pumpkin purée). You can also freeze the purée in ice cube trays, to add to pumpkin smoothies or pumpkin oatmeal.

TOMATOES

You will want to roast tomatoes before freezing them. See "How to peel peaches before freezing" (page 23) for how to peel and freeze, omitting the lemon from the second bowl of water.

ZUCCHINI

We've all been given that massive zucchini from a prideful neighbor or perhaps we've grown a bit too many ourselves. A friend gave me this awesome idea to freeze shredded zucchini.

To freeze: Shred the zucchini, using a grater or mandoline, and place in freezer-safe resealable plastic bags in portions that go along with your favorite zucchini recipes, such as zucchini bread or muffins. You can also use it mixed in with pasta, such as in the Shrimp and Zucchini Spaghetti (page 162).

Note: Zucchini is best frozen in vacuum-sealed freezer-safe plastic bags. Some liquid may come out as you seal the bags.

Fresh Herbs

Many herbs freeze well. Who knew, right?! There are four main ways I like to freeze herbs. Here are examples of all four.

1. The Lay Out and Freeze Method: This is suitable for such herbs as thyme and sage. Thyme: Run your fingers down the thyme stems, letting the small leaves break off onto a plate or cutting board. Turn on some music because this may take a little time, especially if you have a big thyme plant in your yard as we do. Once you have a good amount (say, 1 or 2 cups), place all the leaves in a single layer on a parchment-lined baking sheet and freeze. Once frozen, transfer to an appropriately sized freezer-safe jar, label, and place back in the freezer. Use them as you would use any fresh herb.

2. The Ice Cube Method (with oil): Parsley is best fresh and not frozen, but if you want to preserve some, you can make an herb oil with parsley and freeze the oil in ice cube trays. Blanch the herb for 15 to 20 seconds in boiling water, pat dry in a towel, then blend with oil (should be about five times as much oil as herbs in weight). Refrigerate overnight, then strain through a fine-mesh strainer. Freeze the herb oil in ice cube trays, then transfer the cubes to a labeled freezer-safe resealable plastic bag. This also works for tarragon, dill, oregano, and other more lightweight and feathery herbs.

3. The Ice Cube Method (with oil or water): An easy way to freeze pretty much any herb is to place the herbs, whole or chopped, into ice cube trays, filling two-thirds full. Then fill the rest of the compartments with oil (a blend of olive and grapeseed works well) or water. Freeze the ice cubes then place in labelled freezer-safe plastic bags.

4. The Ice Cube Method (with butter): This method uses melted butter instead of oil, to make herbed butter. Add chopped fresh herbs ($\frac{1}{4}$ cup herbs per $\frac{1}{2}$ cup [1 stick, or 4 ounces] of butter) to room-temperature butter, then freeze in an ice cube tray or in a log wrapped in parchment. After the butter is frozen (24 hours), transfer to a labeled freezer-safe resealable plastic bag. Serve these with fresh bread or add to a casserole or soup.

Ginger

One of my favorite things to freeze is ginger. I used to buy a big ginger root, then only use a quarter or less of it before it went bad in my fridge. Now I leave it in the freezer and just peel, then grate it into a dish or baked good when necessary. Then, back into the freezer it goes. I keep it on my top freezer shelf, where it's easily accessible, and don't put it in a bag, so moisture doesn't get to the root. When I use a bit of the ginger, I try not to keep it out of the freezer for too long, so it doesn't defrost.

Alternatively, you can peel and grate a whole ginger root, then use the Lay Out and Freeze Method (see page 14) to freeze individual teaspoonfuls of the grated ginger to use in smoothies, stir-fries, scones, and so on.

Grated ginger lasts 6 to 8 months in the freezer. If you keep the root whole, it will last longer, though grating and then freezing it is more convenient.

Nuts freeze really well using the Divide and Portion Method and are ready to use straight from the freezer!

Meat

Both raw and cooked meats freeze well, which is great news if you have a smaller family, like me! Sometimes we don't finish a package of raw meat and I can freeze it in portions that are better suited for our recipes, and other times I have leftover cooked meat that we don't get to and I can freeze that, too. I must say, though, that overall I prefer to freeze cooked meat. Raw meat tends to linger in my freezer and it seems just easier to buy another package than to thaw it out. Anyone else with me on this one? But cooked frozen meat is simple to thaw and reheat and perfect for a quick meal. Either way, use the Divide and Portion Method (see page 15) to freeze the meat, whether raw or cooked, in meal-size portions appropriate for your family. Remember that thawing will take much less time if the product is in a small portion. If freezing raw

meat from the grocery store (say it was on sale and you picked up an extra package), repackage it into freezer-safe containers. To thaw meat, place the packaged meat on a rimmed plate in the refrigerator overnight and use within 3 to 5 days.

BACON

I like to use high-quality bacon since we don't eat that much of it. Just using a little bit per dish means you can afford to spend a little more for better (more tasty) results. Thick-cut peppered bacon is my favorite.

To freeze bacon: Open a package of bacon, keeping the bacon slices layered over one another, and use a sharp knife to cut the bacon horizontally, through all the slices, into 1-inch pieces. This way, when you cook the bacon, you will get 1-inch pieces that you can choose to crumble. Use a vacuum sealer to freeze the sliced strips into small bags. I try to get five or six freezer packs per package of raw bacon. This makes for the perfect portion size to top off soups and side dishes, such as the Smoky Corn and Bacon Chowder (page 98) or the Baked Cracker Mac and Cheese (page 79).

To cook bacon that has been frozen: Let the bacon thaw overnight in the fridge, then cook until crisp in a skillet over medium-high heat.

To thaw quickly and cook: Open up the vacuum-sealed package and place the frozen bacon in a skillet over low heat. Once it has slightly defrosted, you can peel the bacon slices apart and let them cook separately. Increase the heat to medium-high and continue to cook, flipping once, until crisp. Let cool on a paper towel–lined plate.

Rice

TO FREEZE: Spread out the rice on a large, rimmed baking sheet to cool. Let cool completely (you can speed up the process by placing it in the refrigerator). Once cool, use a soft spatula to toss the cooked rice with the remaining tablespoon of oil. Transfer to labeled quart-size freezer-safe resealable plastic bags in portions that make sense for your family. Flatten out the bags, then place in the freezer, lying flat. Once frozen, the bags may be stored upright in a sort of filing system, which saves space.

I can pack 4 cups of cooked rice into a quart-size freezer bag, so this recipe will fill two quart-size bags. I usually cook 1 cup of uncooked rice for my family when we are having rice with our dinner, so a 1-quart bag of cooked rice would equal twice that amount. Bags of rice usually come in 2 pounds, so you would double this recipe to make the whole bag (see note) and that would yield 16 cups of cooked rice.

Frozen rice lasts up to 6 months in the freezer.

NO-WASTE TIPS: If you are just making rice for dinner but have leftovers, follow the same freezing procedure with any leftover rice.

If some rice is stuck to the bottom of the pan, pour a little coconut milk over the top and stir over low heat until it all loosens. Add a little honey or sugar for instant rice pudding.

TO REHEAT FROZEN RICE: Transfer the frozen rice to a microwave-safe container, cover, and heat in 1-minute increments on full power, until the rice is hot. You do not need to thaw the rice before reheating.

White Jasmine Rice

Makes 8 cups cooked rice

This method for cooking rice is just the way our family enjoys it. Of course, you can also cook rice more simply with just water, too. The key to freezing the cooked rice is tossing the cooled rice with oil before freezing. Use this same recipe for brown rice as well.

---

2 tablespoons olive oil, divided	¼ cup white wine (optional)
1 onion, finely diced	4 cups water or vegetable stock*
2 cups uncooked jasmine rice	1 bay leaf

---

1. Set a large pot over medium-high heat. Heat 1 tablespoon of the oil, then add the onion. Sauté the onion for 2 minutes, or until translucent.

2. Using a wooden spoon, stir in the rice, coating it with the oil. Add the wine, if using, and let it mostly evaporate. Add the water and the bay leaf and bring to a boil.

3. Lower the heat to a simmer, cover, and cook for 15 to 20 minutes. (Jasmine rice is usually done at around 15 minutes, whereas brown rice takes the full 20.)

4. Once all the water is absorbed, remove the pot from the heat and cover with a kitchen towel for 5 minutes. Fluff with a fork.

*IF USING VEGETABLE STOCK, YOU MAY USE 4 TEASPOONS OF BOUILLON WITH 4 CUPS OF WATER.

NOTE: Cooking rice in extra-large batches makes it easier to mess up the texture of the grain (often being too sticky or mushy). I recommend having two medium-size pots going at the same time if you want to double this recipe and freeze a large quantity of rice at a time.

No-Soak Black Beans or Chickpeas

Makes the equivalent of 10 to 12 (15-ounce) cans black beans

This recipe comes straight from my friend Lindsey. Her blog, Cafe Johnsonia, is one of my favorites. While her fresh and seasonal recipes always catch my eye, this recipe is an easy one to love. Throw dried black beans or chickpeas in a slow cooker with the other ingredients and you end up with more than 10 cans of beans, plus they taste better and have better texture than what you get from a can.

---

2 pounds dried black beans or chickpeas

2 medium-size yellow onions, quartered

4 garlic cloves

2 bay leaves

1 thyme sprig (if you have it)

10 cups water

1 tablespoon salt

---

1. Sort the beans, discarding any small stones or broken or wrinkled beans.

2. Place the beans along with all the other ingredients in a slow cooker and cook on HIGH for 3 to 3½ hours or on LOW for 6 hours. (The time may need to be adjusted according to your specific slow cooker.)

TO FREEZE: Let the beans cool, then Divide and Portion. About 1½ cups of beans plus their liquid is a good ratio (this is the amount in 1 can of black beans). The cooking liquid of the beans helps them to have a longer freezer life, preventing freezer burn. If you wish to freeze them without any liquid, for using beans in salads, burritos, and so on, you can drain them, then pack them into vacuum-sealed bags, or freezer-safe bags or jars (they will last longer in vacuum-sealed bags). The beans without liquid can be defrosted easily by running under warm water. Beans in their liquid that are stored in plastic bags can be defrosted in a bowl of warm water or overnight in the fridge.

FROZEN BEANS LAST UP TO 3 MONTHS IN THE FREEZER.

NO-WASTE TIP: If you're storing the beans with the liquid, it can be drained off or seasoned when you reheat the beans. Also, the liquid from black beans is great to use for black bean soup; the liquid from chickpeas can be used to thin hummus if it's too thick.

Sauces and Soup

Create an ice-water bath by filling one large bowl with ice water and placing another bowl on top. Cool the hot sauce or soup by pouring it into the top bowl above the ice water. Once cool, use the Divide and Portion Method to freeze the item in amounts that make sense to your family. I like to freeze about 6 cups of soup, to serve four, in a gallon-size freezer-safe resealable plastic bag, or 2- to 3-cup portions in quart-size jars or bags, for smaller lunch portions or gifts.

Tip: For pouring sauce and soup into bags, there's a gadget you can find online called a Hands-Free Baggy Rack. I used to have to ask someone to hold a bag while I poured the foods inside, until finding this handy invention.

Dairy

Overall, I don't freeze many recipes heavy with dairy products, such as cream-based soups. However, there are a few exceptions and specific dairy products that do freeze well. Butter can be frozen for up to 3 months. Hard cheese can be frozen for up to 6 months, but may crumble more when you try to use it. Soft cheese actually freezes well, but lasts only about 1 month in the freezer. For recipes containing more dairy, such as the Maple Raspberry Baked French Toast (page 52), you'll want to bake that within a month of freezing. As for dairy soups, they are freezable, but the consistency of the soup tends to change and the dairy appears separated when you reheat them, so I don't usually freeze those. Casseroles containing dairy seem to fare better than cream-based soups when you freeze and then bake them, keeping their creaminess with no obvious signs of separation in the dairy.

Bread

Fresh bread freezes well. I got into a habit of buying bread from a local bakery, but we couldn't get through a whole loaf without its getting stale, so I will usually freeze half of the loaf right away (not sliced) and reheat it in a low 300°F oven at another mealtime. To freeze the bread, I follow the recommendation of a baker to wrap it tightly first in the brown sack that it came in, then super tight in plastic wrap. If it didn't come in a paper sack, just wrap the bread tightly in plastic wrap.

Cake

Cake also keeps well in the freezer. Make sure to wrap it tightly in plastic wrap. You may also try freezing individual portions of cake, which keeps you from thawing the whole cake at the same time if you want only a portion of it. Cake is best frozen plain without icing or custard fillings. Then, if you choose to add those, you can add them fresh when you serve the cake.

Cookies

Cookies can be frozen either baked or raw. After attending holiday cookie swaps and taking home way too many cookies, I always end up storing away a bag or two in the freezer. Breaking out some holiday cookies around New Year's is perfectly acceptable to me! To store baked cookies, place them in a freezer-safe resealable plastic bag with parchment paper layered between the cookies. For raw dough, you can either freeze prescooped dough, as I explain with the Butterscotch Oatmeal Cookies (page 174) or you can freeze the dough in a log, as with the Sea Salt Chocolate Chip Cookies (page 172).

FREEZER LIFE SPAN

This is a conservative guide to how long foods last in the freezer (per USDA.gov).

FOOD	FREEZER LIFE SPAN
Cooked beef	2 to 3 months
Cooked pork	2 to 3 months
Cooked chicken	4 months
Raw beef	6 to 12 months
Raw chicken	9 to 12 months
Raw pork	4 to 6 months
Raw ground meats	3 to 4 months
Vegetables	1 year
Fruit	1 year
Casseroles	4 to 6 months
Soups	4 to 6 months
Cake, muffins, scones	3 months
Bread, biscuits, waffles	3 months
Cookies	3 months
Ice cream	2 months
Breakfast sandwiches or burritos	1 month
Jam	1 year
Quiche, french toast	2 months
Pizza	1 to 2 months
Rice	6 months
Beans	3 months
Avocados	4 to 5 months
Mashed potatoes	6 months
Mac and cheese	6 months
Meatballs	4 months
Applesauce	8 months
Bacon	1 month
Unbaked fruit pie or pie filling	9 months
Filled pasta	1 to 2 months

BREAKFAST

Flaky Herb Biscuits

Makes 12 regular-size biscuits

Although biscuits aren't really hard to make, I rarely get around to making them. But if I think just slightly in advance and make a batch ahead of time, then, when we're eating soup, such as the Chicken and Sweet Potato Gnocchi Soup (page 97) or Roasted Butternut Squash and Apple Soup (page 102), I can just warm a few of these frozen and precooked biscuits in a low oven for a comforting addition. The herbs, though not necessary, add flavor to whatever you're enjoying the biscuits with, whether it's soup or as the bookends of a breakfast sandwich.

3 cups all-purpose flour,
   plus more for dusting

1 tablespoon baking powder

1 teaspoon sugar

1 teaspoon salt

½ teaspoon cream of tartar

¾ cup (1½ sticks,) butter, cold

1 cup ice-cold milk, plus 1 tablespoon
   for brushing the tops

2 tablespoons fresh herbs (thyme, basil,
   and parsley are a great mix)

1. Preheat the oven to 450°F.

2. In a large bowl, combine the flour, baking powder, sugar, salt, and cream of tartar. Cut the butter into almond-size pieces, then use a pastry blender to cut the butter into the flour mixture or quickly use your fingertips to pinch the butter into the flour mixture (don't take too long with this because your fingers can cause the butter to melt), until the mixture is uniform with coarse crumbs. Make a well in the center of the flour mixture. Add the cold milk all at once. Use a fork to stir the mixture just until it is moist.

3. Turn out the dough onto a lightly floured surface. Knead the dough by gently folding and pressing, just until the dough holds together (the quicker you can do this, the better, so that the butter stays cold, making flakier biscuits). Pat or lightly roll out the dough until it is ¾ inch thick (use a ruler to check). Cut the dough with a 2½-inch round biscuit cutter. Reroll the scraps as necessary until all the dough is cut. Place the dough circles 1 inch apart on an ungreased baking sheet. Brush the tops with the extra tablespoon of milk. Bake for 14 minutes, or until golden brown.

4. The biscuits can be frozen unbaked and baked later, or used to top a potpie. I like to freeze them after they are baked and cooled, for ready-made breakfasts or to accompany soup.

TO FREEZE: *Freeze cooled biscuits in the Lay Out and Freeze Method on page 14. For best quality, baked biscuits last in the freezer for 2 to 3 months.*

TO BAKE FROZEN RAW BISCUITS: *Preheat oven to 475°F. Arrange frozen, uncooked biscuits 1 inch apart on an ungreased baking sheet. Bake for 5 minutes, then turn the heat down to 425°F and bake for an additional 10 minutes or until golden brown.*

TO REHEAT BAKED BISCUITS FROM FROZEN: *Place the frozen biscuits in a preheated 300°F oven for 20 minutes.*

Strawberry Rhubarb Jam

Makes 3 (8-ounce) jars jam

My mom and I share an affection for strawberry rhubarb jam. She introduced it to me and since then my affections have just grown stronger. When we first moved into our home, one of the first things I planted was a rhubarb plant in hopes of making this jam from scratch. Now we get out our jam pot and make this as a yearly tradition.

10 to 12 ounces rhubarb stalks, about 2 cups	2½ cups sugar
2 pounds fresh (or frozen) strawberries, washed and patted dry	2 tablespoons freshly squeezed lemon juice
	Pinch of salt

1. Slice the rhubarb into ¼-inch pieces, as you would celery. Hull, then quarter or slice the strawberries.

2. In a medium-size, heavy-bottomed pot, place the fruit, sugar, lemon juice, and salt. Cook over medium-high heat for 5 minutes, until the juices release and start to boil. Then, lower the heat to a low simmer and cook for 1 hour, or until the mixture is reduced to a thick jam. Don't stir during this step; just periodically make sure the jam isn't burning and wipe down the sides of the pot occasionally with a wet pastry brush, so the sugar doesn't caramelize and stick to the sides. Skim the foam off the top and discard.

3. Blend with an immersion blender for a smooth texture or let cool and blend in a standing blender. Or you can leave the jam's texture as is without blending.

TO FREEZE: Freeze using the Divide and Portion Method on page 15 either into freezer-safe jars or rigid plastic containers. Jam will last 1 year in the freezer and 2 weeks in the refrigerator after thawing.

Jalapeño Peach Jam

Makes 3 (4-ounce) jars jam

Every summer I like to make at least one savory jam. Savory jams are definitely still sweet. They just have a hint of savoriness to them by adding such ingredients as herbs, or in this case, jalapeños. Savory jams are great for quick appetizers. Serve them as a condiment on meat, with a cheese plate and crackers, over warmed cheese, or in little biscuit sliders, such as the Braised Beef Biscuit Sliders on page 80.

3 cups peeled, pitted, and sliced peaches (fresh or frozen) (3 to 4 peaches)

⅓ cup sugar

1 teaspoon olive oil

1 shallot, thinly sliced

1 garlic clove, minced

½ red jalapeño or serrano pepper, chopped

1 teaspoon sherry vinegar

Pinch of salt

1 teaspoon sage, finely chopped (2 to 3 leaves)

1. Combine the peach slices and sugar in a medium-size bowl.

2. Place a saucepan over medium-high heat and add the oil. Once the oil is hot (but not too hot), add the shallot, garlic, and jalapeño. Sauté for 2 to 3 minutes. Add the sherry vinegar, then the peach mixture and any juices in the bowl. Season with a pinch of salt. Simmer for 20 minutes, not stirring, over medium-low heat. You may use a wet pastry brush to wipe down the sides of the pot, so the sugar doesn't caramelize and stick to the sides.

3. Once the flavors are combined, you can choose to purée half of the jam or leave it as is (I like to purée half by transferring it to a bowl or measuring cup, then using an immersion blender; alternatively, you can use a standard blender). Stir in sage.

TO FREEZE: Use the Divide and Portion Method on page 15 in jars, leaving appropriate headspace for expansion in the freezer. I like the smaller jars for this because I tend to use it in a small portion all at once, such as over meat or cheese for an appetizer.

NOTE: Jalapeños and serrano peppers can be frozen whole by the Lay Out and Freeze Method (see page 14). These are great for adding spice to chili, soups, and stews. Alternatively, you can go ahead and chop the jalapeños and freeze them in teaspoonfuls as described on page 28 for grated ginger.

Slow-Roasted Tomato *and* Spinach Quiche

Makes 2 quiches; freeze 1 unbaked and enjoy 1 fresh

I didn't like quiche much until I was enlightened to a "better" quiche at culinary school. The basics of this quiche recipe are ones I'll use forever. Change the add-ins and you have endless quiche recipes on your hands.

1 tablespoon olive oil

1 shallot, finely chopped

4 cups packed spinach

⅔ cup Slow-Roasted Tomatoes (page 209), coarsely chopped

1 dozen large eggs, divided

1½ cups heavy cream, divided

1 cup milk, divided

1 teaspoon salt, divided

¼ teaspoon freshly ground black pepper

⅛ teaspoon freshly grated nutmeg

2 frozen prebaked piecrusts, in their plates (see note)

3 cups shredded Gruyère cheese

1. Preheat the oven to 350°F with a shelf on the middle rack.

2. Heat a large sauté pan over medium heat. Heat the oil, then add the chopped shallot. Sauté for 1 to 2 minutes, or until softened. Add all the spinach and use a wooden spoon to stir as the spinach wilts. Once it is all wilted, transfer to a plate to cool.

3. Chop the Slow-Roasted Tomatoes, getting rid of any tomato skins as you see them. Make one quiche custard at a time: In a 4-cup liquid measuring cup, or a mixing bowl with a spout, mix together six of the eggs with ¾ cup of the cream and ½ cup of the milk, plus ½ teaspoon of the salt, ⅛ teaspoon of the pepper, and half of the nutmeg. Mix well with a whisk to make sure all the egg yolks are broken and incorporated.

4. Take one of the prebaked piecrusts out of the freezer. Layer 1½ cups of the cheese, half of the spinach, and half of the roasted tomatoes in the crust. If you have a wire sieve, pour the custard mixture through the sieve over the cheese and veggies. Don't overfill the crust; leave about ⅛ inch of headspace to the top rim of the crust, so it doesn't spill over. You can also place the pan in the oven on a baking sheet just before adding the custard and slide the rack out just enough to pour the custard into the pie shell (so the custard doesn't spill as you walk it to the oven). Repeat to assemble the second quiche.

5. I like to bake one quiche and freeze the second unbaked. Bake the unfrozen quiche for 50 to 60 minutes, or until the center is set (only about the size of a dime in the very center should still be slightly jiggly).

6. Remove from the oven, let cool slightly, then serve.

TO FREEZE: *Place the second, unbaked quiche in the freezer and freeze overnight. Once frozen, use the Casserole Freeze Method on page 16. Label with the baking instructions: 350°F for 60 minutes, then cover the crust edge with foil and bake an additional 15 to 20 minutes, or until custard is set.*

NOTES: *You may use disposable foil pie plates if you don't want one of your pie plates to be in use in the freezer. Alternatively, you can get reusable pie plates from restaurant supply stores for about $1 apiece, to always have spares on hand.*
I like to prebake my piecrusts using pie weights, to ensure that the bottom is fully cooked. This is a matter or preference; if you want to skip that step, go right ahead.

Maple Nut Granola

Makes about 10 cups granola

I'm a sucker for a good granola and this is by far my favorite. The recipe is my version of a recipe in my first cookbook from a local restaurant called Forage, which gifts a similar granola to its patrons as they are leaving the restaurant for the evening. Eating at Forage is an experience that you think of far beyond breakfast the next morning, but its tasty granola sure does ensure that the memories continue.

4 cups old-fashioned rolled oats

2 cups raw pecan pieces (1 [8-ounce] bag)

2 cups raw sliced almonds (1 [8-ounce] bag)

½ cup hull-less, raw, unsalted pumpkin seeds

½ cup hull-less, raw, unsalted sunflower seeds

½ cup wheat bran or oat bran

1 cup unsweetened coconut flakes

1 tablespoon ground cinnamon

1½ teaspoons salt

¾ cup canola oil

1 cup pure maple syrup

1 tablespoon pure vanilla extract

1. Preheat the oven to 325°F and set out a large, rimmed baking sheet (a half sheet pan).

2. In a bowl, stir together all the dry ingredients, including the salt.

3. Heat the oil and syrup in a saucepan over medium heat until simmering. Remove from the heat and stir in the vanilla. Pour the hot mixture over the dry mixture and stir well to combine.

4. Pour everything onto the baking sheet (see note). Bake for 30 minutes, then turn the pan and slightly stir only the edges, making sure they don't burn. (Don't stir all the granola or you will break it up and not have any clusters of oats.) Bake for another 10 to 15 minutes, or until golden brown.

5. Remove from the oven, let cool, then store half of the granola in an airtight container at room temperature.

TO FREEZE: *Use the Divide and Portion Method on page 15 in plastic bags or rigid containers. The granola stores longer in the freezer and can then be kept for future gifts, brunches, or just everyday breakfasts once the first half gets gobbled up, as it will quickly.*

NOTE: *Two things contribute to this granola having a lot of clusters: using one baking sheet instead of two is key so you get layers of oats and nuts; also, not stirring the granola midway through baking also helps the oats clump together.*

Banana Waffles

Makes 12 waffles

As a dear friend of mine was nearing the due date of her fourth child, together we made a big batch of these banana waffles for her to freeze. After the baby arrived, her whole family enjoyed toasted banana waffles for days with little to no effort. Warm up some of the peanut butter maple syrup for a real treat. This combo is my husband's very favorite waffle condiment, though if you're in a hurry, a smear of peanut butter will do! If you're freezing the waffles, undercook them just slightly under crisp—then they'll toast up perfectly from the freezer.

WAFFLES

2 cups all-purpose flour

1 tablespoon sugar

1 teaspoon baking powder

1 teaspoon baking soda

¼ teaspoon salt

¼ teaspoon ground cinnamon

⅛ teaspoon freshly grated nutmeg

2 large eggs

2 ripe bananas, mashed (about ⅔ cup) (see note)

1 cup milk

¼ cup canola oil

1 teaspoon vanilla extract

PEANUT BUTTER SYRUP

¼ cup peanut butter

½ cup pure maple syrup

1. **Make the waffles:** In a bowl, mix together all the dry ingredients. In a separate bowl, using a mixer fitted with the whisk attachment, whip the eggs until they are doubled in size. Add the mashed banana and whip for another minute. Make a well in the center of the dry ingredients and add the milk, oil, and vanilla. Mix just until combined, then fold in the banana mixture.

2. Use a waffle iron to cook the waffles according to the manufacturer's instructions, but leave slightly underdone if you're planning on freezing them.

3. **Make the syrup:** Heat the peanut butter and maple syrup together in a small saucepan over low heat.

TO FREEZE: Let the waffles cool, then freeze using the Lay Out and Freeze Method (page 14) on a parchment-lined baking sheet. Once frozen, transfer to a labeled gallon-size resealable plastic bag. Toast to reheat and serve.

NOTE: When you find ripe or overripe bananas on sale, you can mash them all and freeze them in an airtight container (in a portion size for your favorite recipe). Banana bread, muffins, or these waffles are all great uses for frozen ripe bananas.

Maple Raspberry Baked French Toast

Serves 10–12 in a 9 x 13 pan, or 2 square 9 x 9 baking dishes, serves 5–6 each

My friend Ann gave me a fabulous tip. She keeps a large bag in the freezer at all times for leftover ends of bread or dry, day-old bread. I adopted her trick and now once my bag of frozen bread gets full, I make this French toast. Even leftover bagels, such as plain, cinnamon raisin, or blueberry, work great. I usually slice the bread into cubes or thin slices before freezing it, so that making this dish is quick and easy. Also, check your local grocery store for day-old bread if you need to supplement whatever bread you have on hand to make a full recipe. This recipe can fill one large baking dish or two smaller square baking dishes. It's a perfect quantity to bake half and freeze the other for later.

FRENCH TOAST

12 cups sliced day-old bread (about 2 pounds)

8 ounces mascarpone or cream cheese (optional)

3 cups frozen raspberries, divided

10 large eggs

1 cup half-and-half

2 cups milk

¼ cup packed light brown sugar

1 teaspoon pure vanilla extract

½ teaspoon ground cinnamon

¼ teaspoon freshly grated nutmeg

⅛ teaspoon ground cloves

¼ teaspoon salt

TOPPING

2 tablespoons salted butter

2 tablespoons pure maple syrup

2 tablespoons light brown sugar

TO SERVE

Powdered sugar

Pure maple syrup

1. **Make the French toast:** Grease two 9-inch square baking dishes or one 9 x 13-inch baking dish with butter or cooking spray. Make one full layer of bread (using about half of the bread) at the bottom of the baking dishes. I usually use the random odds and ends of bread for this, and if I grab day-old bread at the store, I'll use that for the top of the French toast. Use a teaspoon to spoon out small amounts of mascarpone cheese onto the bread (this doesn't need to be spread out). Top this layer of bread with 1 cup of raspberries on each baking dish (2 cups total). Top with the remaining bread.

2. In a large bowl, mix together the eggs, half-and-half, milk, brown sugar, vanilla, spices, and salt. Pour this mixture over the bread. Top with the remaining cup of raspberries.

3. **Make the topping:** Melt the butter, then whisk in the maple syrup and brown sugar. Drizzle this over the unbaked French toast. Refrigerate the pans overnight or freeze.

4. Bake in a preheated 350°F oven for 60 to 70 minutes, or until the custard is set and the top is browned. Check after 45 minutes to see if it's browning too much, as you might need to cover it lightly with foil. Remove from the oven, let cool for 10 minutes, then sprinkle with powdered sugar and serve with extra maple syrup.

TO FREEZE: Use the Casserole Freeze Method (page 16) with the following baking instructions: Bake, straight from the freezer, at 350°F for 70 to 75 minutes, checking after 50 minutes to see whether you need to cover the top with foil to prevent too much browning.

Cherry Almond Smoothie

Serves 2

This smoothie is perfectly filling for a great start to the day. Since I'm an oatmeal kind of gal all winter long, I like to find other ways to get my oats in the morning during the warmer months. Adding the oats here only makes the smoothie more satisfying, while the almond butter and cherries are really what make the drink

---

1½ cups frozen banana slices
  (about 2 small bananas)

2 cups pitted frozen cherries

1 cup vanilla almond milk

¼ cup old-fashioned rolled oats

1 tablespoon almond butter

Combine everything in a blender and blend until smooth.

Sweet Green Smoothie

Serves 2

I tend to go overboard with greens in my smoothie, but this smoothie has just the right balance of greens to fruit and liquid. This smoothie is a favorite around our house. I hope you like it as much as we do.

½ cup frozen pineapple

½ cup frozen peaches

1 cup tightly packed baby spinach

1 cup coconut water or freshly squeezed orange juice

½ teaspoon fresh ginger, grated (optional)

Combine all the ingredients in a blender and blend until smooth.

Chocolate Chip–Hazelnut Pumpkin Bread

Makes 3 loaves

This is my mama's pumpkin bread recipe. It's tried and true, requested by friends and family every year. What I love about it is that one recipe makes three loaves. I usually bake a few batches per season, but with just one batch you can enjoy one loaf immediately, freeze one, and give one away! For this book, I added chocolate chips and hazelnuts, but if you prefer a simpler pumpkin bread, this recipe is perfect without the additions.

1 cup hazelnuts, divided

3 cups sugar

1 cup canola oil

4 large eggs, beaten

15 ounces pumpkin purée (page 27), or 1 (15-ounce) can pure pumpkin

3½ cups all-purpose flour

2 teaspoons baking soda

1 teaspoon baking powder

1 teaspoon freshly grated nutmeg

1 teaspoon ground cinnamon

½ teaspoon ground cloves

2 teaspoons salt

⅔ cup water

2 teaspoons pure vanilla extract

2 cups mini chocolate chips (1 [10-ounce] bag)

1. Grease three standard (8½ x 4½ or 9 x 5) loaf pans or disposable foil loaf pans with cooking spray and preheat the oven to 350°F.

2. Use a food processor or high-powered blender to roughly chop ¾ cup of the hazelnuts (they should be like a coarse flour) and use a sharp knife to just barely chop the other ¼ cup. Set the hazelnuts aside. In a stand mixer fitted with the whip attachment, mix the sugar and oil until well combined. Add the beaten eggs and pumpkin to the sugar mixture. Mix well and scrape down the sides and bottom of the bowl to make sure everything is incorporated.

3. In a separate bowl, combine the flour, baking soda, baking powder, nutmeg, cinnamon, cloves, salt, and the ¾ cup of processed hazelnuts. Add the water to the pumpkin mixture alternately with the flour mixture while the mixer is on low speed. Once combined, stir in the vanilla and chocolate chips.

4. Pour equal parts of batter into each loaf pan, each to about ¾ full. Place the pans in the oven. About 45 minutes into the baking, sprinkle the reserved ¼ cup of chopped hazelnuts on top of the loaves to toast (they'll stick to the top and not sink into the loaves at this point). Bake for 50 to 55 minutes total, or until a toothpick inserted into the center comes out clean.

TO FREEZE: *After the loaves are finished baking, remove from the oven and let them cool. Use the Casserole Freezing Method on page 16.*

TO THAW: *Sweet bread can be thawed in the refrigerator overnight, or on the counter for a few hours.*

Zucchini Cherry Muffins

Makes 24 muffins

We like to throw shredded zucchini in just about anything from pasta dishes to muffins. These muffins are perfectly sweet with a hint of cinnamon and make for a great weekday muffin any time of year.

1½ cups pitted frozen cherries

4 cups all-purpose flour

2 teaspoons baking powder

2 teaspoons baking soda

2 teaspoons ground cinnamon

½ cup granulated sugar

½ cup packed brown sugar

¼ teaspoon salt

1 to 1½ cups buttermilk

3 large eggs

2½ cups grated zucchini

½ cup (1 stick, 4 ounces) salted butter, melted and cooled

OPTIONAL STREUSEL TOPPING

¼ cup salted butter, melted

¼ cup light brown suger

¼ cup flour

¼ cup walnuts, chopped

1. Prepare 2 standard-size muffin trays with liners or cooking spray. Preheat the oven to 350°F. Slice the frozen cherries in half and place back in the freezer on a large plate or cutting board, spread out in a single layer.

2. In a large bowl, mix together the flour, baking powder, baking soda, cinnamon, granulated and brown sugars, and salt. In a smaller bowl, mix together 1 cup of the buttermilk and the eggs, zucchini, and melted butter. Make a well in the center of the dry ingredients, then add the wet ingredients. Using as few stirs as possible, stir the wet ingredients into the dry. If the mixture is too dry, add up to the remaining ½ cup of buttermilk. Fold in the frozen cherries.

3. Scoop into the prepared muffin tins, filling almost all the way full. Combine all the ingredients for the optional streusel, if desired. Sprinkle with the optional streusel.

4. Bake for 25 to 30 minutes, or until a toothpick inserted into the center of a muffin comes out clean.

TO FREEZE: Use the Lay out and Freeze Method on page 14, then transfer to gallon-size resealable plastic bags.

TO REHEAT: Warm in a low oven or toaster oven for 10 minutes, or microwave in 10-second bursts until warm. You can also defrost these overnight by placing the frozen muffins on the counter at room temperature in a covered cake or pastry stand.

Honey Nut Sticky Buns

Makes 4 pans of 9 buns each

My friend Haley and I developed this recipe together and it's proof that two minds are better than one. This is an ode to our grandmothers, who both served us honey buns when we were children. Also, as fans of Pioneer Woman's big-batch cinnamon rolls, we knew we wanted to come up with a similar breakfast bun that could be made as a large batch and given to friends and family as gifts or enjoyed at a big holiday brunch. The genius part of this recipe is that it can be made in advance and just baked on the day you want to enjoy them, so that you're not rolling them up when it's a busy time and you can still enjoy them hot from the oven. And no icing is required, because the honey glaze on the bottom of the rolls makes the buns perfectly sweet and gooey.

DOUGH

1 pint whole milk

½ cup canola oil

½ cup sugar

1 (2¼-teaspoon) packet active dry yeast (do not use quick-rise yeast)

4½ cups all-purpose flour, divided, plus more for dusting

½ teaspoon baking soda

½ teaspoon baking powder

1 teaspoon salt

HONEY GLAZE (MAKES 4 CUPS)

1 cup (2 sticks, 8 ounces) salted butter

1 cup honey

1 cup heavy cream

1 cup water

1 teaspoon salt

NUT FILLING

4 cups pecans, chopped

1 cup (2 sticks, 8 ounces) salted butter, at room temperature

¼ cup sugar

¼ teaspoon freshly grated nutmeg (optional)

⅛ teaspoon ground cloves (optional)

1. **Make the dough:** Preheat the oven to 375°F.

2. Place the milk, canola oil, and sugar in a medium-size saucepan over medium heat. Bring to just before a boil (scald), then remove from the heat. Transfer to a bowl and place in the fridge for 15 minutes (set a timer if you think you may forget).

3. Once the mixture has cooled to about 100°F, sprinkle the yeast over the milk mixture. Let sit just 1 minute, then stir in 4 cups of the flour. Cover with a towel and set in a warm place to rise for 1 hour, or until doubled in size (may take longer than 1 hour if the house is cold). Meanwhile, make the honey glaze and the nut filling.

(continued)

4. **Make the honey glaze:** Wash out the saucepan from the dough and combine all the glaze ingredients in the pan. Heat over medium heat until melted and combined. Set aside.

5. **Make the nut filling:** Toast the pecans in the preheated oven for 6 to 8 minutes, or until fragrant and toasted but not burnt. In a medium-size bowl, combine the butter with the sugar, spices, and pecans. Add ¼ cup of the honey glaze. Turn off the oven.

6. **Assemble the buns:** Have ready four 9-inch square foil baking dishes or four 9-inch-diameter foil pie pans. Pour the remaining glaze about ¼ inch deep in each. You may have leftover glaze. Once the dough is finished rising, punch it down, then add the remaining ½ cup of flour along with the baking soda, baking powder, and salt. Mix well to combine.

7. Prepare a large work surface by dusting with flour. Divide the dough into two portions. Roll out one portion into a 12 x 16-inch rectangle. (If you're having trouble rolling out the dough, it may need to rest for 15 to 20 minutes or so; then it should roll out easier and not shrink.) Spoon half of the nut filling over the dough and use a spatula to spread it evenly. Roll the dough tightly in a long roll, starting with a long edge. Cut into 1-inch rolls and place in the glaze-filled baking dishes, 9 buns in each. Repeat with the second portion of dough. To bake without freezing, let the buns rise again for 1 hour, or until doubled, preheating the oven to 375°F at the halfway point, then bake for 16 to 18 minutes.

TO FREEZE: Use the Casserole Freezing Method on page 16.

TO BAKE FROM FROZEN: Remove the plastic and let the buns thaw overnight at room temperature, covered with a kitchen towel. In the morning, bake in a preheated 375°F oven for 16 to 18 minutes.

Ginger Peach Scones

Makes 8 scones

Ginger forms strong opinions. My affections for ginger quickly connected me with a new friend one spring. Some people come in and out of your life so quickly, but you're somehow better for knowing them. I met Sara Ann as she house-sat for a friend of ours who was working in Nepal. While she was just in town for a few weeks, we shared several recipes, among which was her recipe for ginger scones. Sometimes a love for ginger and good food quickly buds a friendship.

1¾ cups all-purpose flour, plus more for dusting peaches and knife

3 tablespoons granulated sugar

2½ teaspoons baking powder

½ teaspoon salt

½ teaspoon grated fresh ginger (see page 28 for how to freeze fresh ginger)

⅓ cup (5⅓ tablespoons) salted butter, cold

1 large egg, beaten

½ cup heavy cream, plus more for brushing

¾ cup frozen peaches (unthawed)

¼ cup chopped crystallized ginger

2 tablespoons coarse sugar, for dusting scones

1. Preheat the oven to 400°F and get out a cookie sheet. Keep the peaches in the freezer until right before you need to mix them in.

2. In a large bowl, mix together the flour, granulated sugar, baking powder, salt, and fresh ginger. Cut in the cold butter with a pastry cutter or by cutting the butter into small, almond-size cubes then using your hands to quickly combine the butter into the flour until pea-size granules are formed.

3. Stir in the egg. Slowly add the cream, adding just enough that the dough leaves the sides of the bowl, starting to form a ball. Chop the frozen peaches and toss them with 1 tablespoon of flour. Quickly but gently stir in the crystallized ginger and floured frozen peaches (quickly so the peaches don't thaw).

4. Pat the dough into an 8-inch circle on the ungreased cookie sheet. Cut into eight wedges with a sharp knife that has been dipped in flour, but do not separate the wedges. Brush with a little additional cream and sprinkle with the coarse sugar. Bake for 20 to 24 minutes, or until golden brown. Remove from the oven and let cool slightly before serving or allow to cool completely before freezing.

TO FREEZE: Once cooled, use the Wrap and Bag Method on page 16 to freeze. These are nice to package individually if you would like to grab and reheat a single breakfast. Reheat in a low oven or microwave in 10-second bursts until warm. You can also defrost these overnight by placing the frozen scones out on the counter in a covered cake or pastry stand.

Breakfast Sandwiches

Makes 8 sandwiches

My husband and I once went on a river rafting trip with a few good friends. I'll never forget the meals we enjoyed along the river or the crazy rapids we endured. Our trip began with some breakfast sandwiches similar to those my friend Heidi made and delivered to each of our cars as we caravanned to the river. These are a perfect beginning to any adventure.

8 bacon slices (see note)
6 large eggs
½ teaspoon salt
⅛ teaspoon freshly ground black pepper

8 Flaky Herb Biscuits (page 39) or English muffins
8 slices of Gouda cheese, sliced into squares just slightly larger than the biscuits

1. Cook the bacon in a large sauté pan over medium heat. While the bacon is cooking, whisk together the eggs with the salt and pepper. Once the bacon is cooked, transfer it to a paper towel–lined plate. Remove the pan from the heat and use a paper towel to swipe up just enough grease from the pan to grease four egg rings or canning jar rings. Discard three quarters of the bacon grease that remains in the pan.

2. Place the pan back over medium heat and set the egg rings in the pan. Once the pan is hot, divide the whisked eggs among the egg rings, filling them about three quarters of the way up. Cook for 4 to 5 minutes, or until you can gently loosen an egg from its ring, using a knife. Remove the rings and flip the eggs over. It's okay if they spill out a little; use a spatula to bring the spilled egg back toward its egg circle. Cook on the second side for just 1 minute. Remove the eggs from the heat and let cool. Repeat.

3. Set out all the sandwich components: biscuits, eggs, cheese, and bacon. Slice the biscuits in half, then layer an egg, cheese, and one slice of bacon broken in half on the bottom half of the biscuit. Place the tops on, then wrap tightly with foil.

TO FREEZE: *Use the Wrap and Bag Method on page 16. Freeze for up to 1 month.*

TO REHEAT: *In a microwave: Unwrap the frozen sandwiches and place on a microwave-safe plate lined with a paper towel (the paper towel absorbs any moisture from freezing so the bread doesn't get soggy). Heat on high for 1 to 1½ minutes, or until the cheese is melted and the egg is warmed through. In the oven: Unwrap the plastic from the sandwiches, then wrap them individually in foil and place in a preheated 350°F oven for 20 to 30 minutes.*

NOTE: *For a veggie-friendly sandwich, instead of bacon, use Slow-Roasted Tomatoes (see page 209) or roasted red peppers and add 1 loose cup of baby spinach, finely chopped, to the eggs before cooking them.*

Breakfast Burritos

Makes 10 burritos

Back in Texas, we grew up frequenting a little breakfast burrito shop. I think I was even tardy to high school on several occasions due to their long drive-thru line. These are just as good as the ones we grew up enjoying and are perfect for a quick breakfast. Make sure you have some extra salsa to dip them into!

2 medium-size russet potatoes, peeled and diced (or 4 cups frozen cooked hashbrowns)

6 bacon slices

10 large eggs

1 teaspoon salt, divided

Olive oil (if necessary)

⅓ cup salsa or Quick and Easy Enchilada Sauce (page 212)

1½ cups shredded sharp Cheddar cheese

10 tortillas (raw tortillas roll up best for frozen burritos)

1. If using frozen, cooked hashbrowns you may skip the step of cooking the potatoes and jump down to cooking the eggs. Place the diced potatoes in a large pot of water, then bring them to a boil. Meanwhile, in a large skillet, cook the bacon over medium-high heat. Once the potatoes are boiling, cook them for another 3 to 4 minutes, or until tender but not falling apart. Drain the potatoes and transfer the cooked bacon to a paper towel–lined plate. Discard about half of the bacon grease, then add the potatoes to the same pan as the remaining grease and sprinkle ½ teaspoon of salt over them. Fry the potatoes for about 10 minutes, or until the edges start to brown and crisp.

2. While the potatoes are frying, whisk all the eggs together. Once potatoes are done, drain off any excess water and transfer them to a big bowl. Add a little oil to the pan, if necessary, and then add the whisked eggs. Scramble the eggs, then transfer them to the bowl of potatoes. Add the salsa and crumbled bacon to the bowl and stir to combine.

(continued)

3. Set up your burrito-rolling station: a flat surface for rolling, a small bowl of water to help seal the burritos, a bowl of shredded cheese, and the big bowl of the egg mixture. If using raw tortillas, heat the tortillas individually by placing them on a hot, dry skillet for 30 seconds per side. (I like to fill and wrap the burritos as the next tortilla is heating up, but be careful not to burn your tortillas.) Scoop ½ cup or more of the egg mixture onto a heated tortilla. Add 2 tablespoons of shredded cheese, then roll it up by folding the two sides in, then rolling from an unfolded edge into a cylinder. To get a good seal on bottom edge of the tortilla, paint a little water along it before completing the roll.

TO FREEZE: *Use the Lay Out and Freeze Method (page 14) on a parchment-lined baking sheet; then Wrap and Bag (page 16).*

TO REHEAT: *Unwrap the burritos and place them on a paper towel in the microwave. Heat on high for 1½ to 2 minutes, flipping halfway through. To crisp the tortilla, place the warmed burrito in a small skillet over high heat and toast for 20 to 30 seconds per side. This extra step is well worth the little effort!*

APPETIZERS AND SIDE DISHES

Mexican Rice

6 cups cooked rice

I made this rice for the first time recently and the first thing I thought of was: I have to freeze some of this! This rice is perfect for quick burrito bowls, an easy lunch or dinner. We even like it for breakfast with black beans and a fried egg.

1 tablespoon olive oil, plus 1 tablespoon for freezing

1 onion, chopped

2 serrano peppers or 1 jalapeño, seeded and chopped

2 cups uncooked long-grain white rice

3 garlic cloves, minced

1 (14.5 ounce) can diced tomatoes

2 cups chicken stock (page 202)

Juice from 2 limes

¼ cup fresh cilantro, chopped

1. Heat a medium-size saucepan over medium heat. Heat the oil, then add the onion and peppers and sauté for 2 minutes. Add the rice and stir, coating the rice with oil. Add the garlic and cook for 1 more minute. Stir in the tomatoes, then add the chicken stock. Bring to a boil, then lower the heat to a simmer. Cover and cook for 15 minutes. Remove from the heat and let rest, covered, for 5 minutes. Fluff the rice with a fork. Add the lime juice and cilantro before serving.

TO FREEZE: *Spread out onto a large-rimmed baking sheet to cool. Let cool completely (you can speed up the process by placing it in the refrigerator). Once cool, use a soft spatula to toss the cooked rice with 1 tablespoon of oil. Then Divide and Portion (page 15) into plastic bags. Flatten out the bags and remove any excess air, then place in the freezer, lying flat to freeze.*
For best quality, frozen rice lasts up to 6 months in the freezer.

TO REHEAT FROZEN RICE: *Transfer the frozen rice to a microwave-safe container, cover, and heat in 1-minute increments on full power, until the rice is hot. You do not need to thaw the rice before reheating it.*

Mexican Rice *and* Black Bean Bowls *with* Avocado Crema

Serves 4

I once went on a bean and rice binge and somehow convinced my husband to eat only rice and beans with me for a full week, as we were trying to save money and live simply (as many do all over the world). He quickly tired of my idea, but after resting from the simple meal for a few months, this continues to appear on our dinner tables.

4 cups Mexican Rice (page 73) or cooked grain of your choosing

2 cups No-Soak Black Beans (page 33)

1 recipe Avocado Crema (recipe follows)

Toppings of your choice—we like Cheddar cheese, black olives, sliced green onions, fresh cilantro, and lime wedges

1. Set out all the ingredients, then have your family members build their own bowls according to their preferences.

Avocado Crema

Makes about 1½ cups crema

1 cup frozen puréed avocado, thawed, or 1 ripe avocado, peeled and pitted

⅓ cup Greek yogurt or sour cream

½ teaspoon ground cumin

¼ teaspoon salt

2 teaspoons freshly squeezed lime juice

1. Blend everything together, using a blender or food processor. Serve immediately over rice and bean bowls, enchiladas, or burritos.

NOTE: Refer to page 20 to learn more about freezing fresh avocado.

Mashed Potatoes *with* Caramelized Onions *and* Roasted Garlic

Serves 12

I love this recipe because it takes plain mashed potatoes and really dresses them up with lots of flavor. Because of the intensity of the onions and garlic, you don't need as much dairy and the potatoes thus have a longer freezer life. These mashed potatoes go great with the Slow-Cooked Beef Short Ribs (page 111) or could be used in a shepherd's pie.

1 whole garlic bulb

1 tablespoon + 1 teaspoon olive oil, divided

5½ to 6 pounds russet potatoes (about 8 potatoes)

2 medium-size yellow onions, thinly sliced

1 tablespoon light brown sugar

1 tablespoon red wine (optional)

½ cup salted butter

½ cup sour cream

½ cup shredded Parmesan cheese

1 cup milk

1 teaspoon salt

½ teaspoon freshly ground pepper

1. Preheat the oven to 425°F. Peel the outer layer of skin from the garlic bulb and slice off the top. Brush the exposed part with the teaspoon of olive oil. Wrap the whole bulb in foil and bake for 30 to 35 minutes.

2. Meanwhile, peel and quarter the potatoes. Place them in a large pot of cold water and bring to a boil. Lower the heat to a simmer, cover, and cook for 15 to 20 minutes, or until soft.

3. Meanwhile, heat the remaining tablespoon of olive oil in a large sauté pan over medium-low heat (nonstick pans do *not* work well for this, but if that's all you have, then plan on its just taking a little longer to caramelize the onions). Add the onions and caramelize for 20 to 25 minutes, stirring occasionally. About halfway through, add the brown sugar and red wine. Once the onions are golden brown, remove from the heat and let cool. Once cool, transfer to a cutting board and roughly chop.

4. Once the potatoes are done cooking, drain, then place in a large bowl. Into the same bowl, squeeze out the roasted garlic and add the chopped onions, butter, sour cream, cheese, milk, salt, and pepper. Beat until mashed and well combined.

TO FREEZE: Let cool. Then Divide and Portion (page 15) or Casserole Freeze (page 16). We like to do 2- to 3-cup portions in quart-size bags, then a couple of small disposable loaf pans able to hold 4 cups of mashed potatoes. For that method, we wrap the containers tightly with plastic wrap, then foil and label the top.

TO REHEAT: Thaw in the refrigerator overnight, then place in a slow cooker on low to reheat. Once warm, turn the slow cooker to warm until ready to serve. Thawed mashed potatoes may also be warmed in a large pot over low heat, stirring every few minutes.

For best quality, mashed potatoes last 6 months in the freezer.

Baked Cracker Mac and Cheese

Serves 10

I have a baked mac and cheese recipe on my blog that gets so much love that I knew I had to share a similar recipe with you. This is a simpler version that I think is even better because of the crisp and buttery crackers crumbled on top. When we make this, we eat half of it the night I make it and freeze the second half. It's easy to make a full meal out of by adding some steamed Classic Veggies (see page 24) and cooked crumbled frozen bacon on top (see page 31 for notes on cooking frozen bacon).

1 pound macaroni pasta

6 tablespoons (¾ stick, or 3 ounces) butter, divided

3 tablespoons all-purpose flour

2 cups milk

2 cups half and-half

4 cups shredded cheese (half white Cheddar and half Gruyère, about 3 ounces each)

1 tablespoon Dijon mustard

¼ to ½ teaspoon salt

¼ teaspoon freshly ground black pepper

⅛ teaspoon freshly grated nutmeg

2 cups crumbled butter crackers

1. Cook the pasta for about 1 minute less than the package directions. Grease two 9 x 9-inch baking dishes with cooking spray or butter (use disposable foil containers, if freezing).

2. While the pasta is cooking, melt 3 tablespoons of the butter in a large saucepan over medium heat. Once melted, sprinkle the flour over the butter and whisk to incorporate. Stir constantly for 1 minute, or until the mixture has the aroma of fresh bread. Then, slowly add the milk and half-and-half, whisking in between additions. Cook for 10 minutes, or until slightly thickened to a sauce, stirring occasionally to prevent sticking to the bottom. Add both cheeses, the Dijon, and the seasonings. Taste and the adjust seasonings as needed. Pour into the prepared baking dishes.

3. Rinse out the saucepan and dry, then place back over medium heat. Add the remaining 3 tablespoons of butter and melt. Once melted, add the cracker crumbs and stir to coat. Cook just until toasted, about 1 minute. Top the macaroni with the crackers, then bake or freeze. Bake in a preheated 350°F oven for 20 minutes, or until bubbly. Let stand for 5 minutes, then serve.

TO FREEZE: Let cool. Then use the Casserole Freeze Method on page 16. Label the top with these baking instructions: Remove plastic, then recover with foil; bake at 350°F for 1 hour; remove foil for the last 20 minutes.

For best quality, mac and cheese will last up to 6 months in the freezer.

Braised Beef Biscuit Sliders *with* Jalapeño Peach Jam

As a local food writer, I get spoiled by trying out local restaurants and events. Many of our meals out inspire my home cooking for the blog and for my family. I had a bite at an event called Taste of the Wasatch that then inspired this bite. I hope it's as memorable for you as it was for me.

8–10 Flaky Herb Biscuits (see note)

1 cup Slow-Cooked Beef Short Ribs (page 111), thawed (see note)

2 tablespoons barbecue sauce

2 to 3 tablespoons Jalapeño Peach Jam (page 43)

1. Preheat the oven to 450°F. Make the biscuits according to directions on page 41, except use your smallest biscuit cutter to form 1-inch-diameter sliders. Bake the tiny biscuits for 8 to 10 minutes, or until browned on top. Place the meat in a skillet over medium-low heat. Add the barbecue sauce and heat until warmed through. Top the hot biscuits with the beef, then add 1 teaspoon of Jalapeño Peach Jam (page 43) to each slider. Serve warm as an appetizer.

NOTES: *Tiny biscuits can be made in advance, then frozen. Rewarm frozen biscuits in a 350°F oven for 8 to 10 minutes. You may also thaw the biscuits overnight at room temperature in a covered pastry or cake stand.*

To thaw the beef, you can place it in the fridge overnight. In a pinch, I place frozen meat in a skillet over low heat and break it apart as it thaws.

Sweet *and* Spicy Cranberry Relish

Makes 2½ cups relish

For several years in a row we celebrated Thanksgiving with another fellow Texan family also living in Utah. One year my friend Bekah made her mom's cranberry relish and we all devoured it! It's perfectly sweet and spicy and can be made in advance, then frozen in preparation for the holidays. The touch of heat from the jalapeño was the perfect reminder of our Texas roots! If you have any leftover from the big holiday feast, serve this with leftover turkey and herbed biscuits or on turkey sandwiches.

1 (12-ounce) bag fresh cranberries
1 cup sugar
Juice and zest of 1 lime

1 red jalapeño or serrano pepper, seeded and finely diced
¼ large red onion, diced

1. Place the cranberries, sugar, lime juice, and lime zest in a food processor and pulse just until the cranberries are shredded. Add the jalapeño and red onion and pulse just a few more times to combine. Let sit for 15 to 20 minutes at room temperature, to let sugars dissolve (the sauce will start to get more juicy when the sugar is dissolved).

TO FREEZE: *Divide and Portion (page 15) into plastic bags and lay flat in the freezer. The cranberry relish will last 2 months in the freezer. To thaw, place in the fridge overnight or submerge the frozen bag of sauce in a bowl of cold water.*

Yogurt- *and* Granola-Filled Peaches

Serves 1

After freezing several batches of peaches late one summer, this became one of my son's favorite snacks. The treat can easily be made into a light dessert using vanilla ice cream (page 168) instead of yogurt.

½ frozen peach (see page 23)

1 heaping scoop plain Greek yogurt (about 2 tablespoons)

1 tablespoon Maple Nut Granola (page 46)

1 teaspoon honey or pure maple syrup

1. Microwave the frozen peach half on a microwave-safe plate in 10-second bursts on high for 20 to 30 seconds total. Top the peach with yogurt, granola, and a drizzle of honey.

NOTE: *To change this snack into a dessert, use the Vanilla Ice Cream (page 168) instead of Greek yogurt.*

Yogurt-Covered Berries

Makes 8 (½-cup) portions

I really became aware of the lack of healthy snack food once I became a mother. I'm always looking for fun snack ideas that are made with real ingredients and simple to put together. My son loves yogurt and berries separately, so this was an easy win for all of us. Plus, it's fun to make with his help, too. These bites are best enjoyed when they're out of the freezer for 20 minutes or so and are great to take on short hikes or for a family picnic.

4 cups assorted berries   **1 cup vanilla yogurt (not Greek)**

1. Wash the berries and let dry on a tea towel. Line a baking sheet with parchment paper. Dip each berry into the yogurt, swirling to coat every side. Let the kids dip and swirl the berries alongside you. Place the dipped berries on the parchment paper.

TO FREEZE: *Once all berries are dipped, place baking sheet in the freezer to freeze using the Lay Out and Freeze Method (page 14). Once frozen, transfer to snack-size bags (pint size), ½ cup in each.*

Ginger Pork Wontons

Makes 18 to 20 wontons

The pork made on page 112 with just a few added ingredients makes for the perfect wonton filling. You can make a big batch of these and always be ready for party appetizers.

1 cup Slow-Cooked Pulled Pork
   (page 112)
1 teaspoon grated fresh ginger (page 28)

1 tablespoon soy sauce
1 tablespoon chopped fresh chives
20 wonton wrappers

1. In a small bowl, combine all the ingredients, except the wrappers.

2. Clear off a work surface area, line a baking sheet with parchment, and fill a small bowl with water to seal the wontons. Lay out several wrappers at a time and scoop out 1 heaping teaspoonful of the pork mixture onto each wrapper.

3. Paint the edges of the wrapper with water, then fold in half, forming a triangle (or forming a half-moon if your wrappers are circles). Then, paint the two edges of the triangle with more water and fold up each side twice (making two small creases over each edge). Once sealed, transfer to the prepared baking sheet. Repeat with the remaining filling and wrappers.

TO FREEZE: Use the Lay Out and Freeze Method (page 14) on a parchment-lined baking sheet, then transfer to a plastic bag.

TO COOK FROM FROZEN: Pour canola or grapeseed oil into a large sauté pan, to a depth of about ¼ inch. Heat over high heat. Once the oil is hot, carefully add the wontons (this may need to be done in batches) and cook on the first side for 2 to 4 minutes, or until starting to brown, then flip and cook for an additional minute.
   Serve the warm wontons with extra soy sauce and chopped chives.

Mozzarella-Stuffed Meatballs

Makes 24 meatballs; serves 6 for dinner or 10 to 12 as an appetizer

When I was first married, my mother-in-law gave me a few recipe cards of her son's favorite meals. Some were more detailed than others. Her Swedish meatball recipe was a favorite of all her boys. On my first attempt of making them, I made one big, now humorous, mistake of cooking the meat before trying to form the meatballs. Years later now, I can laugh at my mistake, especially when we're enjoying meatballs as good as these!

1 pound ground beef

½ cup grated Parmesan cheese

3 garlic cloves, minced

1 tablespoon fresh parsley, finely chopped

½ teaspoon dried oregano

½ teaspoon dried basil

½ teaspoon salt

⅛ teaspoon freshly ground black pepper

½ cup panko breadcrumbs

1 large egg

Pinch of red pepper flakes (optional)

1 tablespoon water

12 small balls mozzarella cheese (about 4 ounces), cut in half (see note)

4 tablespoons neutral oil (grapeseed or canola)

1. Line a baking sheet with parchment paper and get out a plastic cutting board.

2. Place all the ingredients, except the mozzarella cheese and oil, in a medium-size bowl. Use your hands to gently combine but do not overmix (overmixing makes the meat tough).

3. On the plastic cutting board, press the meat mixture into an 8 x 10-inch rectangle ½ inch thick. Use the back of a spoon to make 24 indentions in the meat in 4 x 6 rows. Place a mozzarella ball half into each indentation. Use a sharp knife to cut the meat rectangle into 24 squares. Roll up each square around its mozzarella.

4. About halfway through rolling, heat the oil in a large skillet over medium-high heat and preheat the oven to 400°F. Once all meatballs are rolled, carefully place in the hot oil. Brown for 2 to 3 minutes, then flip and cook for another 1 to 2 minutes on the second side. Transfer to the prepared baking sheet and finish cooking in the oven for 8 minutes.

TO FREEZE: *Use the Lay Out and Freeze Method (page 14).*

TO REHEAT FROM FROZEN: *Heat in sauces on the stovetop or in a preheated 350°F oven for 10 to 15 minutes, or until hot in the middle. Or you can microwave the meatballs for 3 to 4 minutes on high in a single layer with a little water at the bottom of a microwave-safe plate, or in a slow cooker with sauce.*

Serve with tomato sauce as an appetizer or with spaghetti and tomato sauce for a full meal (see page 200 for my Classic Tomato Sauce recipe).

For best quality, the meatballs will last up to 4 months in the freezer.

NOTE: *Alternatively, you may use ½-inch cuts of mozzarella cheese sticks if fresh mozzarella balls are unavailable where you live.*

Slow Cooker Applesauce

Makes about 8 cups

Last year I got a huge box of Honeycrisp apples from a local orchard. We consumed as many as we could, but when they started to get a little soft, I made a huge batch of applesauce. I made half on the stovetop and the other half in a slow cooker. The stovetop sauce burned the bottom of my pan so badly it took a week for me to revive it. From now on, I'll always make applesauce in my slow cooker.

6 pounds apples (about 12 apples),
   cored and quartered*

½ cup water or apple cider

2 teaspoons freshly squeezed
   lemon juice

½ teaspoon ground cinnamon

¼ teaspoon freshly grated nutmeg

⅛ teaspoon ground cloves

1. Place all the ingredients in a slow cooker and cook on LOW for 6 hours, stirring after 3 hours, then every hour after. Purée in a blender or food processor. Let cool before freezing.

* I keep the skins on when I make applesauce, but feel free to peel your apples before quartering them. Once you purée the sauce, the apple peels are unnoticeable.

TO FREEZE: *Use the Divide and Portion Method (page 15) or Ice Cube Method (page 16) in muffin tray.*
   When thawed, the applesauce will last for a couple of weeks in the fridge. For best quality, applesauce lasts 8 months in the freezer.

SOUPS

Chicken and Sweet Potato Gnocchi Soup

Serves 8; serve half and freeze half

This soup demands a brisk winter day to match. It's a simple comforting chicken soup, the kind we like to have on a sick day. The sweet potato gnocchi make it extra comforting and they don't even need to be thawed before adding them to the soup. If you don't have sweet potato gnocchi in your freezer, you can use regular gnocchi, cooked noodles, or rice. If you're freezing the soup, store it without the gnocchi or noodles and add those right before serving.

1 tablespoon olive oil

1 medium yellow onion, diced

4 large carrots, sliced

4 celery stalks, sliced into ¼-inch pieces

10 cups Chicken Stock (page 202)

4 cups cooked chicken (roasted from page 115 or rotisserie)

1 teaspoon fresh parsley

1 teaspoon fresh sage

1 teaspoon fresh rosemary

1 teaspoon salt (see note)

⅛ teaspoon freshly ground black pepper

2 cups Sweet Potato Gnocchi (unthawed) (page 216) or other frozen gnocchi

1. In a large stock pot, heat up the olive oil. Add the onion, then the carrot and celery. Sauté for 2 to 3 minutes, then add the chicken stock and bring to a low simmer. Add the chicken, herbs, and seasonings. At this point you can remove half of the mixture if you're freezing half. Right before serving, add the sweet potato gnocchi while the soup is over medium-high heat. The gnocchi will rise to the top of the pot when they are done cooking (taste one to check doneness). Serve with extra chopped herbs on top.

TO FREEZE: *Cool the hot soup over an ice-water bath (fill one large bowl with ice water and place the soup in another bowl on top), then use the Divide and Portion Method (page 15). Half of this recipe would be a good fit for a 1-gallon bag and serves four.*
For best quality, this soup will last 4 to 6 months in the freezer.

NOTE: *You may use less salt, depending on whether you use homemade stock or store-bought. If using a store-bought, I would go with low-sodium, then adjust the salt to your liking.*

Smoky Corn **and** Bacon Chowder

Serves 8; serve half and freeze half

This soup idea was the first to pop into my mind when I thought of soups for this book. The only problem was I had no idea how I was going to make it. I ended up combining smoked paprika and the technique of slightly toasting corn cobs for a toasted corn broth, to create a pure smoky flavor to the soup. This one is wonderful served with the Flaky Herb Biscuits on page 39.

4 ounces frozen bacon pieces (page 29)

1 onion, diced

4 garlic cloves, minced

6 waxy potatoes (Yukon gold or red potatoes work well), cubed

4 cups corn

1 red bell pepper, seeded and chopped

1 teaspoon salt

1 tablespoon smoked paprika

¼ teaspoon dried thyme

¼ teaspoon dried basil

¼ teaspoon dried oregano

¼ teaspoon red pepper flakes

8 cups vegetable stock or smoky corn cob broth (see note)

1 cup half-and-half

TO FREEZE: *Cool the hot soup over an ice-water bath (fill one large bowl with ice water and place the soup in another bowl on top), then use the Divide and Portion Method (page 15).*

For best quality, this soup will last 4 to 6 months in the freezer.

NOTE: *You can use vegetable stock, but if you'd like to enhance the smoky flavor in the soup, try making smoked corn broth during corn season (at the same time as you're freezing corn). Reserve corn cobs as you're shucking corn for the freezer, then turn your broiler to* HIGH. *Place the cobs on a sheet pan on the top level of your oven and let broil for 30 seconds to a minute, then rotate the cobs until each side has a little browning. Placed the browned (but not burnt) cobs in a large stockpot with water and bring to a boil. Lower the heat to a simmer and cook for 1 hour, or until broth has a slightly yellow tinge and tastes of smoked corn. Prepare an ice-water bath by setting one bowl in a slightly larger bowl filled with ice. Strain the stock into the top bowl. Discard all the cobs. Freeze the stock in gallon-size freezer-safe resealable plastic bags or in rigid plastic containers.*

1. Cook the bacon over medium heat in a large stockpot. Once the bacon is cooked and the fat from the bacon is rendered or released, transfer just the bacon from the pan to a paper towel–lined plate to cool. Add the onion and garlic to the bacon grease and sauté for 2 minutes. Add the potatoes and cook for 5 minutes, stirring occasionally with a wooden spoon to get anything that might be stuck to the bottom of the pan. Add the corn, bell pepper, salt, and all the herbs and spices and continue to cook, stirring occasionally, for 5 minutes. Add the vegetable stock and use a wooden spoon to scrape the bottom of the pot (anything that might be stuck to the bottom will actually just add more smoky flavor to the soup). Cook for 15 to 20 minutes, or until the potatoes are soft but not falling apart.

2. If freezing half, separate it now before adding the half-and-half and it will preserve better. Stir the half-and-half into the pot, then continue to cook for just a couple more minutes, or until warmed through. Remove from the heat and serve with the bacon pieces.

Tomato Basil Soup

Makes 6 servings (about 12 cups total)

My mother used to take me to this little French bistro back in Texas while I was growing up. It had the best tomato basil soup. As the restaurant expanded, it started to sell the soup in jars. On a few occasions, my mom sent me a jar or two when she visited. This is a riff on that special soup. My favorite use for this soup is to pack it into jars and freeze it. Then, when I have a sick friend, I defrost the soup and bring a jar over.

¼ cup + 1 tablespoon olive oil, divided

6 garlic cloves, finely chopped

2 (28-ounce) cans whole peeled tomatoes (I like to use one fire-roasted and one plain)

4 cups tomato juice

2 cups vegetable stock (use 2 teaspoons vegetable bouillon [page 207] with 2 cups water)

1 teaspoon salt

½ teaspoon freshly ground black pepper

½ cup packed fresh basil leaves, plus more for garnish

1 cup heavy cream

¼ cup (½ stick, 2 ounces) salted butter

1. In a large stockpot, heat the 1 tablespoon of oil. Add the garlic and sauté over medium heat for 2 minutes. Add the tomatoes, juice, vegetable stock, salt, and pepper, then bring to a simmer. Cook at a low simmer for 30 minutes, adding the basil after 20 minutes. Blend, using an immersion blender, or let cool and then blend in a standing blender. Stir in the heavy cream, butter, and remaining ¼ cup of olive oil.

2. Serve with fresh basil and toasted bread or grilled cheese.

TO FREEZE: *Cool the hot soup over an ice-water bath (fill one large bowl with ice water and place the soup in another bowl on top), then use the Divide and Portion Method (page 15).*
For best quality, this soup will last 4 to 6 months in the freezer.

NOTES: *Try a Thai version by using Thai basil and coconut milk instead of the cream.*
This is also great as gifts: Portion 2 cups per jar into six pint-size freezer-safe jars (leaving ½ inch of headspace at the top of the jars). Share the fresh soup with friends or freeze the jars to give to friends when they are sick.

Roasted Butternut Squash *and* Apple Soup

Makes 8 servings (about 16 cups total)

Butternut squash soup trumps all other fall soups, in my opinion. Roasting the squash and adding roasted apples makes for a sweet and toasty version of this classic favorite. And once you sample the roasted apples, you might just have a new favorite fall snack!

2 medium-size butternut squash

2 tablespoons + 1 teaspoon olive oil, divided, plus more to roast squash

1 teaspoon salt, plus more to roast squash

⅛ teaspoon freshly ground black pepper, plus more to roast squash

5 large sweet apples, cored

1 sweet onion

3 celery stalks, sliced into ¼-inch pieces

6 cups vegetable stock

1 bay leaf

3 whole cloves, or a pinch of ground cloves

1 tablespoon fresh thyme, or 1 teaspoon dried

1 tablespoon fresh parsley, or 1 teaspoon dried

1 tablespoon fresh sage, or 1 teaspoon dried

1 cup apple cider

1. Preheat the oven to 400°F and get out two rimmed baking sheets.

2. Cut the squash in half lengthwise and remove but do not discard the seeds (see note). Discard the stringy insides. Brush the cut side with olive oil and sprinkle with salt and pepper. Place cut side down on one of the baking sheets and place the baking sheet in the oven. Carefully pull out the oven rack just enough that you can pour a ¼-inch depth of water into the baking sheet. Make sure the water also gets under the squash halves. Roast for 1 hour, or until soft and a fork goes through easily. Slice the apples into eight slices per apple and toss with 1 teaspoon of the olive oil. Place these on the second baking sheet in a single layer (not overlapping) and roast for 40 minutes, or until tender, tossing halfway through.

3. Once the apples and squash are both cooked, remove from the oven and let cool.

4. Sauté the onion and celery with the 2 tablespoons of oil. Scoop the squash from its skin and add to the onion mixture. Add three quarters of the apples and stir, mashing slightly with a wooden spoon. Add the vegetable stock, bay leaf, and cloves, along with the salt and pepper, and bring to a simmer. Simmer for 15 to 20 minutes, then add the herbs. Cook for another 5 minutes, then remove the whole cloves, if using, and the bay leaf. Blend, using an immersion blender, or let cool and blend in a standing blender. Stir in the apple cider and return to the heat to warm through. Adjust the seasonings to taste. Serve with the remaining roasted apple wedges.

TO FREEZE: Cool the hot soup over an ice-water bath (fill one large bowl with ice water and place the soup in another bowl on top), then use the Divide and Portion Method (page 15).

For best quality, this soup will last 4 to 6 months in the freezer.

NOTE: To toast the squash seeds, rinse them, then pat dry with a paper towel. Toss with 1 teaspoon of oil and 1 teaspoon each of ground cinnamon and sugar (more or less, depending on how many seeds you're roasting—sometimes I remove a portion to toast plain, just for garnishing the soup, before discarding the rest). Toast for 15 to 20 minutes in a preheated 400°F oven, stirring halfway through, or until browned and crisp.

Turkey and Black Bean Chili

Makes 10 to 12 servings

This recipe is my version of a favorite from a local ski resort. While the expert chefs at this slope keep their recipe secret, as they should, I have had fun trying to make a copy to enjoy at home. This is great to have in the freezer for those snow days when you are outside making snowmen or sledding and want to come home to something warm and hearty. Place the frozen chili in a slow cooker on LOW if you're going to be away or thaw overnight and warm up in a stockpot over low heat.

3 tablespoons olive oil, divided

2 pounds turkey breast meat, diced

2 tablespoons salted butter

1 yellow onion, diced

½ red onion, diced

4 garlic cloves, minced

2 jalapeño peppers, seeded and chopped

3 celery stalks, sliced into ¼-inch pieces

1 large bell pepper, seeded and diced

⅓ cup masa harina (corn flour)

1 tablespoon ground Mexican oregano

1 tablespoon ground coriander

1 tablespoon chili powder

2 tablespoons cumin

2 tablespoons light brown sugar

1 teaspoon salt

5 cups Chicken Stock (page 202) or vegetable stock using bouillon (page 207) and olive oil

2 cups No-Soak Black Beans (page 35) or 1 (15-ounce) can, drained and rinsed

2 cups frozen sweet corn (see page 24)

Optional garnishes: cheese, green onions, fresh cilantro, sour cream

1. Heat 1 tablespoon of the oil in a large stockpot over medium-high heat. Add the turkey meat and sear for 5 minutes on one side, or until lightly browned. Flip and cook for 2 more minutes. Remove the turkey meat from the pot and set aside. Add the remaining 2 tablespoons of oil and the butter to the pot. Add the onions, garlic, jalapeños, celery, and bell pepper. Sauté for 5 minutes.

2. Meanwhile, combine the corn flour with all the spices as well as the brown sugar and salt.

3. Once the onions are translucent, add the spice mixture to the onion mixture and stir with a wooden spoon. Cook for 3 to 5 minutes, or until the spices are fragrant. Add the stock slowly, using the spoon to scrape up any brown pieces from the bottom of the pan. Bring to a simmer and add the turkey, black beans, and corn. Simmer for 25 minutes. Serve with cheese, green onions, cilantro, and sour cream.

TO FREEZE: Cool the hot chili over an ice-water bath (fill one large bowl with ice water and place the chili in another bowl on top), then use the Divide and Portion Method (page 15).

For best quality, this soup will last 4 to 6 months in the freezer.

Tuscan White Bean Soup
with Sausage *and* Kale

Serves 6 to 8

After visiting the Tuscany region of Italy years ago, I have made several versions of this soup. This particular version is extra hearty with the Italian sausage. This soup, similarly to the Chicken and Sweet Potato Gnocchi Soup (page 97), can be made with whatever veggies you have on hand.

1 tablespoon olive oil

1 pound Italian sausage (I like the spicy kind but sweet sausage works well, too)

1 large onion, diced

2 large carrots, diced

2 celery stalks, diced

1 teaspoon salt

½ teaspoon dried thyme

¼ teaspoon dried rosemary

¼ teaspoon freshly ground black pepper

3 (15-ounce) cans cannellini beans (6 cups), drained and rinsed

1 (15-ounce) can diced tomatoes with their juices, or 2 medium-size tomatoes, diced

6 cups chicken stock (page 202)

1 zucchini, diced (optional)

1 yellow squash, diced (optional)

2 cups kale, stemmed, leaves roughly chopped

1. In a large stockpot, heat the oil over medium-high heat. Remove the sausage from its casing and add to the pot. Brown, 3 to 4 minutes per side, not overstirring (so you can get some caramelization and browning on the meat). Add the onion and cook for another 2 minutes, stirring occasionally. Add the carrots, celery, and seasonings. Cook for 5 more minutes. Add the beans and tomatoes. Use a wooden spoon to scrape up any browned bits from the bottom of the pan. Add the chicken stock and simmer for 15 minutes. Add the zucchini and yellow squash, if using, and then stir in the kale. Cook the kale for just about 1 minute, or until slightly wilted, then remove the pot from the heat. Serve hot with crusty bread or let cool and freeze in proportions that are fitting for your family.

TO FREEZE: *Cool the hot soup over an ice-water bath (fill one large bowl with ice water and place the soup in another bowl on top), then use the Divide and Portion Method (page 15).*
  For best quality, this soup will last 4 to 6 months in the freezer.

MAIN DISHES

Slow-Cooked Beef Short Ribs

Serves 8

This is a super simple recipe for short ribs. The idea is to make, then freeze the beef in meal-size portions so that you can have shredded beef on hand. The seasoning is simple on the beef, to allow you to use the beef in several different recipes and change the flavor profiles for each. Short ribs are my favorite beef to slow cook, but they don't yield a large quantity in the end, and you may have more mouths to feed than I do. So, if you're looking for a beef cut that has a higher-quantity yield, try using a 4-plus-pound roast beef or boneless short ribs.

4 pounds beef short ribs, bone in	1 tablespoon salted butter
1½ teaspoons salt	1 cup red wine
½ teaspoon freshly ground black pepper	1 cup beef stock (page 204)

1. Use a sharp knife to carefully trim off any silver skin and some (but not all) of the excess fat from the beef. Season all sides of the beef with salt and pepper.

2. Heat a large sauté pan over medium-high heat. Add the butter to the pan and raise the heat to high. Sear the short ribs for 4 minutes, their best side down first. Flip and sear for another 3 minutes. Transfer to a wire rack to let cool slightly. Place the sauté pan back over low heat and carefully add the wine (if it's too hot, it may splatter and steam a little, so be careful). Use the wine to deglaze the pan, scraping up the seasoning from the bottom of the pan with a wooden spoon.

3. Pour the pan juices into a slow cooker along with the beef stock. Add the seared beef with its best side facing up. Cook on LOW for 8 to 10 hours, depending on your slow cooker. The meat will fall apart easily when it's ready. You can serve some fresh that day and shred the rest and freeze for later uses.

TO FREEZE: *Let the meat cool, then use the Divide and Portion Method to freeze (see page 15). I like to freeze in 1½- or 2-cup portions. Cooked meat freezes best in vacuum-sealed bags.*

Slow-Cooked Pulled Pork

Serves 8 to 10

This is the easiest pulled pork recipe that you'll find and because it is uncommitted in flavor, you may use it in several different ways, from tacos to soup or barbecue sandwiches. The key is to start with a high-quality pork that doesn't need a lot of extra seasoning as well as to first sear the pork before slow cooking it.

4 pounds pork shoulder

1 teaspoon salt

¼ teaspoon freshly ground black pepper

1 tablespoon salted butter

¼ cup vegetable stock

1. Rub the meat with salt and pepper on all sides.

2. Heat a large skillet over high heat. Place the butter in the hot pan. Once the butter is melted, add the pork shoulder and sear on each side (about 4 minutes per side). The exterior of the meat should be medium to dark brown.

3. Pour the vegetable stock into a slow cooker, then place the seared pork on top. Cook on LOW for 7 to 8 hours (depending on your slow cooker), then shred.

TO FREEZE: *Let the meat cool, then use the Divide and Portion Method to freeze (see page 15). I like to freeze in 1½- or 2-cup portions. Cooked meat freezes best in vacuum-sealed bags.*

Roasted Chicken

About 3 cups cooked shredded chicken

This is my very favorite recipe for roasted chicken. It may seem too simple, but that's the glory of it. The skin is perfectly seasoned and slightly crisp, while the meat is juicy and tender. Thanks to the famous Thomas Keller from whom I adapted this recipe.

1 (3-pound) farm-raised chicken (see note)	1 tablespoon kosher salt 1 teaspoon freshly ground black pepper

Preheat the oven to 450°F. Rinse the chicken, then pat dry well with paper towels, inside and out. Season the exterior and interior of the bird evenly with salt and pepper. Place the chicken in a large, oven-safe sauté pan or a roasting pan. Roast until it has an internal temperature of 165°F, 50 to 60 minutes. Remove from the oven and let rest for at least 15 minutes before cutting or shredding. It is easiest to pull the meat off the bones when the bird is still warm.

TO FREEZE: Let the meat cool, then use the Divide and Portion Method to freeze (see page 15). I like to freeze in 1½- or 2-cup portions. Cooked meat freezes best in vacuum-sealed bags.

NOTES: You can also shred chicken from a store-bought organic rotisserie chicken.
   If you haven't tried roasted grapes yet, you must. Add them around the roasting chicken about halfway through its cooking time. Serve the chicken with roasted grapes over warm polenta.

Beef and Potato Hand Pies

Makes 6 to 8 large hand pies or 12 to 16 small pies

My friend Heather is originally from England and when I asked her what food she misses most of her home country, she easily replied, "Meat pie." While savory pies are definitely not as common here in America, after making these, I'm not sure why they aren't! These beef hand pies are like being able to hold on to while simultaneously sink your teeth into a beef stew jacketed in flaky piecrust. These are great for lunches in the smaller portions or great as hearty dinners with a large green salad to pair.

2 medium-size russet potatoes, peeled and diced into ½-inch cubes

2 cups shredded Slow-Cooked Beef Short Ribs (page 111)

6 to 8 sun-dried tomatoes, minced, or 1 tablespoon tomato paste

1 teaspoon Worcestershire sauce

1 teaspoon Dijon mustard

¼ cup beef stock (page 204)

¼ cup red wine (or extra beef stock)

¾ teaspoon salt

¼ teaspoon freshly ground black pepper

All-purpose flour, for rolling out the dough

1 unbaked Pie Dough (page 167), thawed overnight in the fridge

1 large egg, for egg wash

Sea salt (optional), for sprinkling

Crushed black peppercorns (optional) for sprinkling

1. Place the cubed potatoes in a large pot of water and bring to a boil. Once boiling, cook until tender but still holding their shape, 3 to 5 minutes.

2. In a large skillet, combine the beef, tomatoes, Worcestershire sauce, Dijon, beef stock, wine, salt, and pepper and stir. Cook just until the liquid is absorbed, 3 to 5 minutes. Adjust the seasonings to taste.

3. Line a large baking sheet with parchment paper. Dust a work surface with flour and keep a small bowl of extra flour beside you as well as a small bowl of water. Divide the piecrust dough into four or eight equal-size balls, depending on whether you are making small or large pies. Keep one of the balls out and place the rest back in the fridge. Roll out the ball into a 4- to 5-inch-diameter disk for a small pie, or an 8-inch-diameter disk for a large one. Use a pizza cutter or knife to trim off any jagged edges, making a smooth circle of dough (see note).

4. Fill the small pie with ¼ cup of the beef mixture or the large pie with ¾ cup of it. Use your fingertips to brush water on the edges of the dough. Fold over one side of the dough, making a half-moon shape. Seal the edges by using the tines of a fork to press down into the dough. Use a sharp knife to slit three airholes in the top of the pie. Place the filled pie on the prepared baking sheet and then into the fridge. Repeat with the remaining dough and filling, refrigerating the pies as you form them. Freeze or bake.

5. When you're ready to bake, whisk the egg. Use a pastry brush or your fingertips to brush the top of the pastry with the egg wash. Top the pie with a little sea salt and crushed black peppercorns (optional). Bake in a preheated 375°F oven for 45 minutes, or until golden brown.

TO FREEZE: *These pies can be frozen before or after baking, using the Lay Out and Freeze Method (see page 14), then the Wrap and Bag Method (see page 16).*

TO BAKE FROM FROZEN: *Bake for 50 to 60 minutes, until golden brown.*

NOTES: *Use water to patch the pie dough if you have any holes or uneven edges, as you make the circles for each pie.*

Don't be shy about using flour as you roll out the dough. Sprinkle with flour every once in a while as you're rolling it out and occasionally flip the dough over, making sure it's not sticking to the bottom of your surface. Add more flour to your work surface anytime the dough looks moist or has absorbed all the flour. If you're worried about the dough's tasting like flour, once you have your shape, use a pastry brush to brush off any excess flour from the dough.

Moroccan Chicken *and* Apricot Stew

Serves 8 to 10; serve half and freeze half

My quest for the perfect Moroccan stew recipe started after I visited a Moorish area of Spain. I had the best Moroccan stew while sitting at a table surrounded by people I would now call longtime friends. The stew was slightly sweet with warm spices and was served over couscous with pine nuts. This is my reinvention of that perfect meal and it just so happens to freeze perfectly well.

3½ to 4 pounds chicken thighs, bone in

1 teaspoon salt, plus more for sautéing chicken

Freshly ground black pepper, for sautéing chicken

3 tablespoons olive oil, divided

1 large or 2 medium-size sweet onions, diced

4 garlic cloves, minced

2 tablespoons all-purpose flour

2 teaspoons paprika

2 teaspoons ground cumin

1 teaspoon ground cinnamon

1 teaspoon ground ginger

2 (14.5 ounce) cans diced tomatoes (fire-roasted if you can find it)

2 cups chicken stock (page 202), or 1 (14-ounce) can low-sodium

1 cup dried apricots, quartered

2 cups No-Soak Chickpeas (page 35) or 1 (15-ounce) can, drained and rinsed

Juice of ½ lemon

1. Remove and discard the skins from chicken thighs and sprinkle with salt and pepper. Place a large sauté pan over medium-high heat. Heat 2 tablespoons of the olive oil. Sear the chicken, 3 to 4 minutes per side, until browned (you may have to do this in batches, depending on the size of your pan). Remove the seared chicken from the pan, transferring to a plate.

2. To the same pan, add the remaining 1 tablespoon of oil along with the diced onion and sauté or 2 to 3 minutes, or until translucent. Add the garlic and sauté for another minute. Stir together the flour and all the seasonings. Sprinkle this mixture over the onion and stir with a wooden spoon to combine. Cook the flour mixture for 1 minute, or until fragrant.

3. Add the diced tomatoes and bring to a simmer. Stir, using a wooden spoon to scrape up any browned bits from the bottom of the pan. Cook for 5 minutes, then add the chicken stock, apricots, and chickpeas. Squeeze the lemon juice over a wire-mesh strainer to catch any seeds. Remove any seeds you can see from the lemon and toss the lemon half into the stew as well. Simmer for 25 minutes. Serve with couscous or rice and pine nuts.

TO FREEZE: Use the Divide and Portion Method (see page 15) to freeze.

Chicken, Black Bean, and Corn Enchiladas

Makes 20 enchiladas; serve half and freeze half

No freezer cookbook would be complete without an enchilada recipe. For this book, I wanted to incorporate a lot of the other frozen components from the book, such as black beans, corn, and homemade enchilada sauce. Although you can surely just buy these ingredients at the store, the fully homemade version does make the dish better! When my friend Bekah and I made these, we doubled both the enchilada sauce recipe and the enchilada recipe and made 6 to 8 casserole dishes of these to bring to friends.

2 cups cooked and shredded chicken (page 115)

2 cups No-Soak Black Beans (page 35), or 1 (15-ounce) can, drained and rinsed

2 cups corn, thawed if using frozen (see page 24)

2 cups sharp Cheddar cheese (or a Mexican blend of cheese), divided

2 cups Quick and Easy Enchilada Sauce (page 212), divided, plus more if needed

20 flour tortillas

1. In a large bowl, combine the chicken with black beans, corn, 1 cup of the cheese, and about ½ cup of the enchilada sauce.

2. Get out two rectangular foil baking dishes. Warm the tortillas slightly in a 300°F oven or microwave for 15 to 30 seconds on high to make them more pliable. Scoop about ⅓ cup of the chicken mixture into a tortilla and roll up. Lay seam side down in a baking dish. Repeat with the remaining chicken mixture and tortillas. Pour the remaining 1½ cups of enchilada sauce over the enchiladas, using slightly more if needed. Top with the remaining cup of cheese.

3. If baking right away, bake in a preheated 350°F oven for 20 minutes.

TO FREEZE: *Use the Casserole Freeze Method to freeze (see page 16) to freeze. Label with the following: remove plastic before baking; bake at 350°F for 45 minutes,.*
Serve with fresh cilantro and avocado. This is a great example of mixing fresh with frozen. When you top a once frozen dish with a few fresh ingredients, such as cilantro and avocado, it really helps brighten up the flavors.

Pork Tacos with Chimichurri and Avocado Slaw

Serves 4

Similarly to the Orange Sesame Beef Stir-Fry (page 133), this recipe is not one that is frozen as a whole but all its components are easy to freeze, so that when you're ready to make these tacos, they can be enjoyed in a matter of minutes.

AVOCADO CREMA SLAW
½ cup Avocado Crema (page 74)
½ cup shredded green cabbage
½ cup shredded red cabbage
½ cup shredded carrot

FOR ASSEMBLY
1½ to 2 cups Slow-Cooked Pulled Pork, thawed (page 112)
½ cup Chimichurri (page 211)
8 corn tortillas, warmed in the oven

1. **Make avocado crema slaw:** Toss the avocado crema with the shredded cabbage and carrots.

2. **Assemble the tacos:** Heat the thawed pork over low heat in a skillet as the tortillas are warming up. Layer the tacos with the avocado crema slaw, then the pork, then the chimichurri sauce. Serve the tacos with Mexican Rice (page 73) or black beans (page 33).

Sweet Potato Black Bean Burritos

Makes 12 burritos

Freezer burritos are a lifesaver when it comes to lunches. These burritos with sweet potatoes and black beans are our favorites. Sometimes I also add cooked chicken to the mixture. The real secret to great freezer burritos is using freshly cooked raw tortillas so they roll well. If you like your burritos a little crispy, after you heat a frozen burrito in the microwave, you can place it on a dry skillet for 20 to 30 seconds per side and it will crisp the tortilla just perfectly. Serve these with salsa.

ROASTED SWEET POTATOES

4 large sweet potatoes, peeled and diced into ½-inch cubes

2 tablespoons olive oil

1½ teaspoons salt

¼ teaspoon freshly ground black pepper

FOR ASSEMBLY

4 cups No-Soak Black Beans (page 35), or 2 (15-ounce) cans, drained and rinsed

½ cup Quick and Easy Enchilada Sauce (page 212)

2 cups shredded sharp Cheddar cheese

12 tortillas (see note)

1. **Roast the sweet potatoes:** Preheat the oven to 400°F and cover a large baking sheet with foil. Toss the diced sweet potatoes with the oil, salt, and pepper. Place on the prepared baking sheet. Roast the sweet potatoes for 30 minutes, or until soft and starting to caramelize and brown on the edges. You should have about 6 cups of roasted sweet potatoes.

2. **Assemble the burritos:** Combine the roasted sweet potatoes with the black beans and enchilada sauce.

3. Prepare a work station with the sweet potato mixture, a small bowl of shredded cheese, and a large cutting board for rolling the burritos.

4. If you're using raw tortillas, heat a large skillet over medium-high heat. Warm the tortillas for 15 to 30 seconds per side. I like to warm them individually as I'm filling and wrapping them.

5. Fill one cooked tortilla as you're warming the next tortilla (being careful not to burn the heating tortilla as you're working). Fill with about ¾ cup of the sweet potato mixture, then top with 1 to 2 tablespoons of the cheese. Fold the ends up toward the center, then roll one edge up over the filling and finish rolling tightly to seal (see note). Repeat with the remaining ingredients and tortillas.

NOTES: *The raw tortillas cooked right before rolling seem to seal better than the precooked ones do. You can find the raw kind at most grocery stores now, in a refrigerated section.*

To help seal the burritos I keep a small bowl of water beside me and paint the edge of the tortilla with water as I'm rolling it up.

TO FREEZE: *Use the Wrap and Bag Method (see page 16) to freeze.*

TO REHEAT: *Unwrap the burritos and discard the plastic wrap. Place them on a paper towel in the microwave for 2 to 2½ minutes on high, flipping halfway through. To crisp the tortillas, place the warmed burritos on a small, dry skillet over high heat and toast for 20 to 30 seconds per side. This extra step is well worth the little effort!*

Falafel

Makes 32 falafel balls

After buying frozen falafel from a grocery store, I knew I had to try making it at home. After you do the work of making and forming the falafel balls, these are so great to have around. If you bake them right away, then freeze, you can literally take them out in the morning and they'll be thawed by lunchtime for a great on-the-go, kid-friendly lunch or snack. If you are at home, take the extra few minutes to make some tzatziki sauce and serve them with warmed pita bread.

6 ounces baby spinach

2 tablespoons olive oil, divided

½ cup breadcrumbs, plus more for rolling the falafel

¼ cup all-purpose flour

4 cups No-Soak Chickpeas (page 35), or 2 (15-ounce) cans, drained and rinsed

¼ red onion or 1 large shallot, diced

2 teaspoons ground cumin

2 tablespoons freshly squeezed lemon juice (1 lemon)

1 teaspoon salt, plus more for rolling the falafel

⅛ teaspoon freshly ground black pepper, plus more for rolling the falafel

⅛ teaspoon red pepper flakes

1 large egg

1. Line two baking sheets with parchment paper.

2. In a large sauté pan, sauté the baby spinach in 1 tablespoon of the oil until wilted, then set aside to cool. Combine all the ingredients, except the egg and spinach, and including the remaining tablespoon of oil, in a large (8-cup) food processor bowl. Process until smooth. Squeeze out any excess liquid from the spinach, then roughly chop. Add the spinach to the food processor and pulse just a few times to incorporate into the chickpea mixture.

3. Roll the mixture into balls about 2 tablespoons each, using a cookie scoop or tablespoon. Use a fork or small whisk to beat the egg. Dip the balls into the egg wash, then roll into extra breadcrumbs and season with salt and pepper. Set the breaded falafel in a single layer on the prepared baking sheets and either bake or place in the freezer.

(continued)

4. To bake, preheat the oven to 375°F. Bake the falafel for 17 minutes, flip, then bake for another 5 minutes, or until lightly browned on both sides. Serve with Quick Tzatziki Sauce (recipe follows), pita bread, and fresh toppings, such as chopped tomatoes, cucumbers, feta cheese, and pickled red onion.

TO FREEZE: *Use the Lay Out and Freeze Method (see page 14) to freeze. You may freeze falafel either cooked or raw. I find it easier to just cook them all and freeze a portion of or all the falafel.*

TO COOK FROM FROZEN: *Bake in a preheated 375°F oven for 20 minutes, flip, then bake for an additional 5 minutes.*

Quick Tzatziki Sauce

Makes 1½ cups sauce

1 teaspoon freshly squeezed lemon juice
½ seedless cucumber, finely diced
1 garlic clove, minced
1 cup (8 ounces) plain Greek yogurt (We like whole-milk yogurt for this.)
¼ teaspoon salt
½ teaspoon fresh dill, chopped

1. In a small bowl, combine all the ingredients. Serve with falafel and pita bread.

Chicken, Chickpea, *and* Spinach Curry

Serves 6

Once I discovered how easy it is to make curry at home, I couldn't stop making it. This recipe is a riff on the traditional chickpeas with spinach dish that you may find in most Indian restaurants. While it is usually a side dish, the addition of chicken makes it perfectly substantial for a main. The basic first few steps of this recipe—melt the butter, sauté the onion with the ginger and garlic, then add the spices—are true for the start of any curry. Adjust the spices and seasonings to your own preferences.

1 tablespoon salted butter or ghee
1 small yellow onion, finely diced
2 garlic cloves, minced
2 teaspoons grated fresh ginger
2 teaspoons curry powder
½ teaspoon ground coriander
½ teaspoon ground turmeric
½ teaspoon ground cumin
¼ teaspoon cayenne pepper

½ teaspoon salt
1½ cups Classic Tomato Sauce (page 200)
1 cup chicken stock (page 202)
3 cups No-Soak Chickpeas (page 33), or 1½ (15-ounce) cans, drained and rinsed
2 cups shredded Roasted Chicken (page 115)
6 to 8 ounces baby spinach
¼ cup heavy cream or half-and-half

1. In a large sauté pan, melt the butter. Add the onion, garlic, and ginger and sauté over low heat for 10 minutes, stirring occasionally. You basically want the onion to almost melt. Add all the seasonings, making a paste with the onion. Stir as the spices toast for 1 minute. Add the tomato sauce and use a wooden spoon to scrape up any bits from the bottom of the pan. Slowly stir in the chicken stock. Add the chickpeas and chicken and cook for just a couple of minutes, until warmed through. Fold the spinach into the mixture, letting it warm and slightly wilt for just 30 seconds to 1 minute. Stir in the cream and remove from the heat. Serve with White Jasmine Rice (page 32). If you let the curry cook down a little, you may need to add a little more tomato sauce or some water to make it saucier.

TO FREEZE: Use the Divide and Portion Method (see page 15) to freeze.

Orange Sesame Beef Stir-Fry

Serves 4

This dish is not one that we freeze, but is perfectly easy to make anytime if you have all the ingredients ready-made in your freezer, when it literally takes no time and effort at all, with only one skillet to clean afterward. If you keep your freezer stocked with those premade ingredients, this is a great regular weeknight meal.

2 tablespoons olive oil

3 cups frozen stir-fry vegetables (see note)

¼ cup water

1½ cups frozen Slow-Cooked Beef Short Ribs (page 111), thawed in the fridge overnight

1 cup Orange Sesame Stir-Fry Sauce (page 214)

4 cups cooked white jasmine rice, rewarmed in the microwave if using frozen (page 30)

1 tablespoon fresh basil, chopped, for garnish

1 tablespoon sesame seeds

1. Place a large skillet over medium heat. Heat the oil, then add the frozen vegetables. Stir them to coat with the oil, then add the water and cover until thawed. Add the beef (if it's still slightly frozen, it will thaw out quickly). Stir in the stir-fry sauce and cook for just a couple of minutes. Divide the rice among four plates, then top with the beef and veggies. Ladle extra sauce over each plate. Garnish with the basil and sesame seeds.

NOTE: You can find stir-fry veggies in the freezer section at most grocery stores or make your own veggie packs (see page 24).

TO FREEZE: Place the pie(s) on a baking sheet in the freezer overnight. Make sure they are sitting evenly on a shelf. Once frozen, use the Casserole Method (see page 16) to wrap and store.

TO BAKE FROM FROZEN: Preheat the oven to 375°F. Place a baking sheet on the lower shelf to catch any drips, then place the pie plate on the middle rack. Bake for 65 to 75 minutes, or until golden brown and bubbly. Let cool for 5 minutes before serving.

NOTES: I like to keep a bag of pearl onions in my freezer just for this use. I think they are perfect in potpies, but of course a diced yellow onion will also do the job!

One pie dough recipe will make more than enough for two potpies made in standard pie plates. Save the extra dough for a small fruit tart or a hand pie!

Chicken Potpie

Makes 2 pies, each serving 4; serve 1 and freeze 1

The uses of piecrust are truly endless. These single-crust potpies contain no dairy (except butter), so they freeze especially well. Feel free to change up the veggies according to the season. Don't forget to slit a few holes in the crust before you bake it, so the crust doesn't get soggy and the filling doesn't bubble over.

2 tablespoons salted butter

2 tablespoons olive oil

1 cup pearl onions (see note), or 1 large onion, diced

4 garlic cloves, minced

5 medium-size carrots, diced small

3 celery stalks, diced small

½ cup all-purpose flour, plus more for dusting

4 cups chicken stock (page 202)

1½ cups frozen peas

3 cups shredded Roasted Chicken (page 115), thawed

¼ cup fresh parsley, chopped

1 teaspoon fresh or frozen thyme (see page 28), chopped

1¼ teaspoons salt

⅛ teaspoon freshly ground black pepper

1 recipe Pie Dough (page 167, or ready-made frozen), thawed overnight in the fridge (see note)

1. Melt the butter in a large sauté pan over medium heat. Add and heat the oil, then carefully add the onions (the frozen pearl onions might pop a little in the hot butter). Sauté the onions for 5 minutes if using pearl onions or 2 minutes for diced onion. Add the garlic and cook for 30 seconds. Add the carrots and celery and cook for 5 more minutes. Sprinkle the flour over the veggies and stir with a wooden spoon to coat the veggies evenly, about a minute. Slowly pour in the stock and stir well to combine as the stock heats. Bring the mixture to a boil, then lower the heat to a simmer and cook for 8 minutes. Add the frozen peas and let them thaw and warm for a couple more minutes. Stir in the roasted chicken, herbs, and seasonings.

2. Pour the filling into two disposable pie plates, leaving just ⅛ inch of space at the top. Let cool while you roll out the pie dough.

3. Remove one of the two dough balls from the fridge and lightly flour a work surface. Roll out the dough to about a 10-inch diameter, adding more flour as needed. Then, trim any uneven edges. Set the dough circle over the cooled potpie

filling. Fold the overhang inward while pinching to crimp the edge. Slit three vents in the top, using a sharp knife. Repeat with the other dough ball, to top the other potpie (see note). Bake right away or freeze.

4. To bake a potpie right away, preheat the oven to 375°F. Place a baking sheet on the lower shelf to catch any drips, then place the pie plate on the middle rack. Bake for 40 to 45 minutes, or until golden brown and bubbly. Let cool for 5 minutes before serving.

Slow-Cooked Turkey Lentil Taco Filling

Makes about 6 cups of taco filling, serving 12 (½ cup each)

My friend Becky, who writes the blog Project Domestication, once shared a recipe for lentil tacos. We loved it so much that it became a favorite. I have now made my own version with a mixture of lentils and ground turkey and we use it in hard-shell tacos as well as in Mountain Taco Salad (page 139). This can quickly be made in a slow cooker, then cooled and frozen for quick taco suppers.

1 pound dried lentils	½ teaspoon red pepper flakes
4 cups vegetable stock	½ teaspoon freshly ground black pepper
1 pound ground turkey	1 tablespoon ground cumin
2 onions (I like 1 red and 1 yellow), diced	1 teaspoon dried Mexican oregano (see note)
4 garlic cloves, minced	1 teaspoon paprika
2 tablespoons chili powder	1½ teaspoons salt
½ teaspoon onion powder	1 cinnamon stick

1. Place the lentils and stock in a slow cooker. Add the turkey along with the onion, garlic, and all the spices and seasonings. Cook on LOW for 5 hours. Stir as needed at the end of cooking to break up the turkey meat.

TO FREEZE: *Remove the cinnamon stick, let cool, then use the Divide and Portion Method (see page 15) to freeze. Two cups is usually plenty for a family of four for tacos or taco salads.*

NOTE: *Use regular oregano if you can't find Mexican.*

Mountain Taco Salad

Serves 4

Over the years we've shared countless meals with friends. This recipe is inspired by my friend Diana, whose mama used to make it for her while she was growing up, and now she continues to make it for her own family. While her taco filling recipe has different ingredients the method is the same: once you have well seasoned the taco filling, pile it high on top of chips and lettuce, then top with your favorite taco additions. Family favorites are always worth stealing . . . thanks, Diana and Lavonne.

1 head of romaine lettuce

2 tablespoons olive oil

1 tablespoon freshly squeezed lemon juice

Salt and freshly ground black pepper

4 cups or large handfuls of tortilla chips

2 cups Slow-Cooked Turkey Lentil Taco Filling (page 136)

1 cup shredded Cheddar cheese

½ avocado, diced

A few radishes, thinly sliced

More topping ideas: green onions, sour cream, red onion, guacamole or Avocado Crema (page 74), salsa, black olives

1. Wash, then chop the lettuce and dress with the oil and lemon juice and season with salt and pepper to taste. On four plates, layer the chips, then the lettuce, and ½ cup of taco filling, then add your desired toppings.

Chicken Pesto Pizza

Serves 4

I'm always looking for more ways to use up the summer pesto from my freezer. This pizza is a perfect way to enjoy both pesto and frozen slow-roasted tomatoes. It can be made with or without chicken, though it is a bit hardier with it. This could also be used as a flatbread appetizer.

½ recipe Pizza Dough (page 215)
Cornmeal, for rolling dough
⅓ cup Any Nut Pesto (page 199) (about 3 frozen cubes), thawed

½ cup shredded Roasted Chicken (page 115) (optional)
⅓ cup Slow-Roasted Tomatoes (page 209)
1 cup shredded mozzarella cheese
Olive oil, for brushing

1. Preheat the oven to 475°F and place a baking stone in the oven, if you have one (though this is not necessary).

2. Roll out the pizza dough on a baking sheet or pizza peel sprinkled with cornmeal. Spread the pesto on the pizza dough, then top with the shredded chicken and slow-roasted tomatoes. Sprinkle the cheese over everything. Brush the edge of the pizza dough with a little bit of olive oil. Transfer to the pizza stone or a baking sheet. Bake for 12 to 15 minutes, or until the cheese is bubbly and slightly brown.

TO FREEZE: *Use the Pizza Method (see page 16) to freeze.*

Sausage *and* Pepperoni Calzones

Makes 8 large or 10 to 12 medium-size calzones

Our love for calzones can be traced back to our home town of Lubbock, Texas, at a little pizza shop called One Guy that serves calzones extra cheesy with a generous amount of sausage and pepperoni inside. And now, many years later, I wouldn't have them any other way!

All-purpose flour, for dusting
20 ounces shredded mozzarella cheese
½ cup Parmesan cheese, grated
1 recipe Pizza Dough (page 215),
    thawed overnight

1 pound Italian sausage
30 slices of pepperoni
3 cups Classic Tomato Sauce (page 200)
Olive oil or melted salted butter,
    for brushing

1. Lightly dust a large cutting board with flour and get out a rolling pin. Line two baking sheets with parchment paper.

2. Prepare a workstation with a small bowl of flour, a small bowl of water, the shredded mozzarella, and the grated Parmesan. Separate the two pizza dough balls into eight equal-size smaller balls, or 12 if you're making medium-size calzones. Place the dough balls on one of the prepared baking sheets and let rest on the counter.

3. Heat a large skillet over medium-high heat. Add the sausage and cook until lightly browned on both sides, about 4 minutes per side. Meanwhile, slice the pepperoni into quarters. Add the pepperoni as well as the tomato sauce to the pan. Let the sauce reduce for about 5 minutes, or until thick and not too liquidy. Remove from the heat and let cool slightly.

4. Take one of the pizza dough balls and roll it out on the floured surface to about 8 inches in diameter for a large calzone or 6 inches for a medium-size one. Use flour throughout the rolling, so that the dough doesn't stick to your work surface. Spoon out about ¾ cup (for large) or ½ cup (for medium) of the sausage mixture onto the bottom third of the dough circle, leaving a clean border around the edge. Top with 3 to 4 tablespoons of mozzarella cheese and 1 teaspoon of grated Parmesan. Use your fingertip to paint a little water around the edge of the dough. Fold the top of the dough over the filling and press to seal. If you have enough dough, you can roll that edge up (simply fold it over

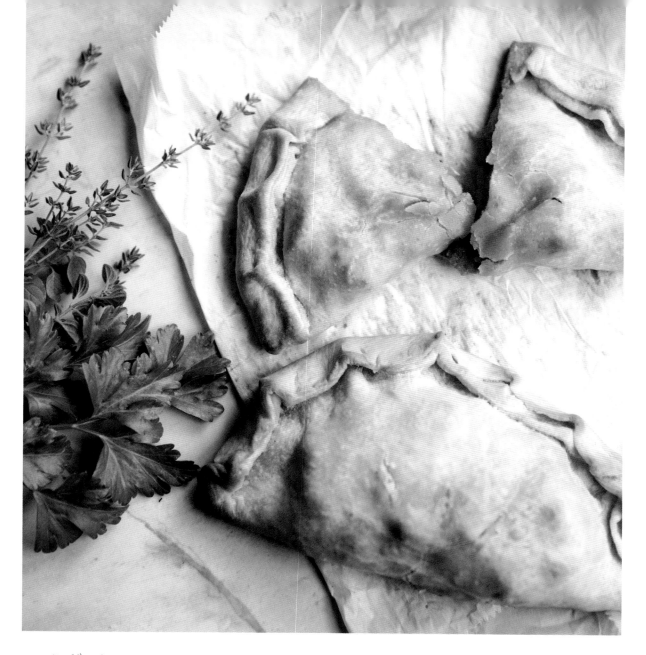

on itself) to form a more secure seal. Crimp the rolled edge with your fingertips as you would with a piecrust, for a nice-looking edge. Set the completed calzone on the other prepared baking sheet. Repeat with remaining dough and filling. You can bake right away or freeze the prepared calzones. Alternatively, you can also freeze baked calzones for a quicker meal.

5. **To bake right away:** Preheat the oven to 450°F. Use a sharp knife to make three slits in the top of the calzones, then brush each calzone with olive oil or melted butter. Bake for 30 to 40 minutes, or until the crust is golden brown.

TO FREEZE: *Use the Lay Out and Freeze Method (see page 14) and then the Wrap and Bag Method (see page 16) to freeze.*

TO COOK FROM FROZEN: *Preheat the oven to 450°F and bake for 45 to 55 minutes.*

Peach Prosciutto Pizza

Serves 4

This is my take on ham and pineapple pizza. Peaches with prosciutto is a combo I enjoy all summer long, whether on pizza, over greens for a hearty salad, or just as an appetizer. This pizza can be made as a main dish, or with thinner crust, as a flatbread appetizer.

Cornmeal, for rolling dough

½ recipe Pizza Dough (page 215)*

¾ cup Classic Tomato Sauce (page 200)

2 cups mozzarella cheese, shredded

1 peach, pitted and thinly sliced, or two frozen halves (page 20), thawed and thinly sliced

4 ounces thinly sliced prosciutto

Olive oil, for brushing

2 cups arugula

Salt and freshly ground black pepper

1 tablespoon aged balsamic vinegar, for drizzling (see note)

1. Preheat the oven to 475°F and place a baking stone in oven, if you have one (though not necessary).

2. Roll out the pizza dough on a baking sheet sprinkled with cornmeal or on a pizza peel, then layer with the tomato sauce, then the mozzarella cheese, peaches, and prosciutto. Brush the edge of the pizza dough with a little bit of oil. Transfer to the pizza stone or a baking sheet. Bake for 12 to 15 minutes. Top with the arugula, then sprinkle with salt and pepper to taste and drizzle with the balsamic.

TO FREEZE: *Use the Pizza Method to freeze before adding the arugula and balsamic.*

NOTE: *For the balsamic vinegar, you want something pretty thick. If the balsamic you have at home is thin, you can reduce it over low heat until it thickens. The aged balsamic that I like to use for this is Villa Manodori.*

*Always make the full recipe for pizza dough and just freeze the other half, or make a freezer pizza ready for the oven.

Sausage *and* Spinach Lasagna

**Serves 16 total (2 large pans serving 8 each or 4 square pans serving 4 each);
serve 1 and freeze 1 or 3**

*When developing a lasagna recipe for this book, I had too many ideas to narrow it
down. There are two big reasons this is the one I chose–sausage and basil ricotta.
I made this one extra cheesy and the creamy mixture of ricotta makes the lasagna
truly dreamy. This makes enough for two big lasagna pans or four square pans.
Baking frozen lasagna does take some time, so do plan ahead, but I promise that
you will never want a lasagna from the grocery freezer aisle again.*

2 pounds Italian sausage

7 cups Classic Tomato Sauce (page 200),
    or 2 (26-ounce) jars marinara sauce,
    divided

2 (16-ounce) packages ricotta cheese

4 large egg yolks

2 teaspoons salt

⅛ teaspoon freshly ground pepper

½ teaspoon red pepper flakes

¼ teaspoon freshly grated nutmeg

1 cup Parmesan cheese, grated

1 cup loosely packed basil, chopped,
    plus more for garnish

2 (1 pound) packages no-boil lasagna
    noodles (you may not use all of them)

1 pound frozen spinach, thawed and
    drained well (squeeze out any extra
    liquid)

2 pounds mozzarella (2 [16-ounce]
    packages), shredded

1. In one extra-large or two large skillets, cook the sausage,
   browning on both sides and breaking apart with a spoon as it
   cooks, about 8 minutes. Once it is cooked, add all but 1 cup of
   the tomato sauce. Lower the heat to a low simmer.

2. In a food processor or high-powered blender, combine the
   ricotta, egg yolks, salt, pepper, red pepper flakes, nutmeg, and
   Parmesan. Add the basil and blend for just a few seconds.

3. Lightly grease two 9 x 13-inch rectangular baking dishes (use
   foil pans for freezing) or four 9-inch square baking dishes.
   Spread ½ cup of the meat sauce over the bottom of each pan.
   Then layer on in this order: noodles (overlapping slightly),
   ricotta mixture, spinach, mozzarella, meat sauce. Repeat the
   layers one more time, starting with the noodles. For the third
   and final layer, add the noodles, then the ricotta mixture, then
   the remaining cup of tomato sauce (without meat), then the
   mozzarella.

Fast to the Table Freezer Cookbook

4. To bake unfrozen, cover with foil and bake in a preheated 350°F oven for 30 minutes, then uncover and bake for 15 more minutes, and finally broil on HIGH for 1 extra minute to brown the cheese on top.

TO FREEZE: *Use the Casserole Method (see page 16) to freeze.*

TO BAKE FROM FROZEN: *Unwrap the plastic and re-cover with foil. Bake, covered, in a preheated 350°F oven for 1½ hours, then uncover and bake for 15 more minutes, and broil on HIGH for 1 final minute.*

Pasta *with* Chicken, Kale, *and* Slow-Roasted Tomato Sauce

Serves 8, or two dinners for 4

As we prepped all day for our culinary school graduation dinner, one of my fellow students quickly whipped up a pasta dish that I'd always remember. She blended some leftover slow-roasted tomatoes from a previous class with a quick béchamel sauce, creating a rich, light-red sauce that we enjoyed with gnocchi. It fueled us for the rest of our workday. I re-created her sauce but paired it with pasta, chicken, and kale for a hearty meal.

1 pound (16-ounce package) dried pasta

2 tablespoons olive oil

½ onion, diced

2 garlic cloves, minced

⅓ cup Slow-Roasted Tomatoes (page 209), chopped

2 tablespoons flour

2 cups milk

2 cups cooked and shredded chicken

1 teaspoon salt

⅛ teaspoon red pepper flakes

½ bundle kale

2 cups reserved pasta cooking liquid

2 cups mozzarella cheese

BREADCRUMB TOPPING:

¼ cup breadcrumbs

1 tablespoon salted butter, melted

2 tablespoons Parmesan cheese

1. Bring a large pot of salted water to a boil, add pasta, and cook according to package directions, taking one minute off the cooking time.

2. Meanwhile, in a blender, blend the oil, onion, garlic, and roasted tomatoes. Heat a large skillet over medium-high heat. Add the tomato mixture to the pan and cook for 2 minutes, stirring occasionally with a wooden spoon.

3. Sprinkle the flour on top and continue to stir for 30 seconds. Pour in milk and whisk to combine. Bring to a low simmer and add the chicken and seasonings.

4. Once pasta is done cooking, reserve two cups of the pasta cooking liquid and drain the rest of the water. Add the kale to the skillet with the chicken and tomato sauce, then top with the cooked pasta—the hot pasta will help wilt the kale. Add the 2 cups of reserved pasta liquid and the mozzarella and stir to

combine. Let simmer for just a few minutes. You can choose to serve this now or serve half and transfer the other half into a foil-disposable baking sheet.

5. Mix the breadcrumbs with the melted butter and parmesan cheese and sprinkle the mixture over the baking dish (use ½ the breadcrumb topping per 9 x 9 square baking dish). If you're serving half without baking, you won't need the whole recipe for the breadcrumb topping—this is only if you're baking the pasta.

TO FREEZE: Use the Casserole Method (see page 16) to freeze. Label the top of the dish and freeze.

TO BAKE FROM FROZEN: Preheat oven to 350°F. Uncover the dish, remove and discard the plastic. Re-cover with the foil and bake in the preheated oven for 1½–1 hour 45 minutes, or until bubbly. Remove foil for the last 10 minutes of baking.

Butternut Squash Ravioli *with* Maple Balsamic Glaze

Serves 6

One of my very favorite dishes I have ever created at home is this butternut squash ravioli. Although the process, especially if you're making your own pasta and not using wonton wrappers, takes a little time and a few extra hands, it is worth the effort. Making homemade ravioli is super fun and having ready-made ravioli in my freezer is definitely my favorite thing to have prepared. If you have a pasta maker, you have no excuses and I promise you'll be glad for the adventure. The filling in this pasta is so tasty that whatever sauce you add needs not to be complex. Even a simple olive oil with salt and pepper will do, though the maple balsamic glaze is simple enough and makes the dish truly magical.

FILLING

2 cups butternut squash, finely diced

1 tablespoon olive oil

2 garlic cloves, minced

1 shallot, finely diced

½ teaspoon salt, divided

⅛ teaspoon freshly ground black pepper, divided

2 cups loosely packed spinach, finely chopped

1 tablespoon fresh parsley, finely chopped (see note)

1 teaspoon fresh sage, finely chopped (see note)

1 teaspoon fresh thyme, finely chopped (see note)

⅓ cup mascarpone cheese (see note)

⅓ cup finely grated mixed Pecorino Romano and Parmesan cheese

DOUGH

1 recipe Pasta Dough (page 218) (see note)

1 large egg, whisked, for sealing the dough

Glaze, recipe follows

1. **Make the filling:** Cut off the top (neck) of the squash, then slice in half. Remove the stem, then turn one of the halves upright (vertical) and use a sharp knife to carefully peel the skin off the squash. Rotate and continue to slice downward to get all the skin off. Once skin is removed, turn the squash flat side down and slice into ⅛-inch half-moons. Turn the slices onto their sides and slice into ⅛-inch strips. Turn the strips horizontally on the cutting board, then cut into ⅛-inch tiny cubes. Use 2 cups of squash cubes for the filling.

2. In a large sauté pan over medium heat, heat the olive oil, then add the garlic and shallot. Sauté for just 1 minute or less, then

(continued)

add the diced squash and continue to cook for 10 minutes, stirring occasionally. Season with half of the salt and pepper. Add the spinach and cook until wilted, about 1 minute, then add the herbs. Transfer the mixture to a medium-size bowl and mix in the cheeses and remaining salt and pepper. Taste and adjust the seasonings as necessary.

3. This can be made 1 day in advance of making the pasta and filling the ravioli. Store in an airtight container in the fridge.

4. **Make the ravioli:** Prepare and fill the ravioli according to the directions on page 219. At this point, you can freeze the ravioli.

TO FREEZE: *Use the Lay out and Freeze Method (see page 14) to freeze raw, filled ravioli.*

NOTES: *Use half of the amount of herbs if you're using dried herbs instead of fresh.*

Cream cheese can be substituted for mascarpone.

Homemade pasta may be replaced with wonton wrappers for an easy and quick alternative to making your own pasta at home. Wonton wrappers cook faster and are more likely to fall apart when cooked in boiling water.

5. **Cook the ravioli:** Place a large pot of salted water over high heat and bring to a boil. While the water is coming to a boil, make the sauce (recipe follows). Once the water is boiling, carefully add the ravioli. Keep the water at a low boil and wait for the ravioli to rise to the surface of the water (that's when you know they're ready). Remove the ravioli from the water with a slotted spoon and transfer to a large serving plate, tossing lightly with oil to prevent sticking. Top with a simple sauce or Maple Balsamic Glaze before serving.

Maple Balsamic Glaze

Serves 4

This sauce, this sauce. It is the best sauce I've made up to date. My husband said the dish as a whole is the best thing that has come from our kitchen. If you make the ravioli ahead of time and freeze them, the whole dish will take you less than 15 minutes to make, which includes making this sauce. Add a nice salad and some crusty bread and you have a beautiful meal to share.

⅓ cup chopped hazelnuts	2 tablespoons pure maple syrup
¼ cup (½ stick, 2 ounces) salted butter	2 tablespoons aged balsamic vinegar (the thicker kind)
12 sage leaves	¼ teaspoon salt

1. Toast the hazelnuts in a preheated 375°F oven for 8 minutes, or until fragrant. Meanwhile, melt the butter over low heat, slowly letting it brown and get bubbly. You'll start to smell a nutty aroma from the browned butter when it's ready. Add the sage leaves and let them gently fry for 30 seconds, then transfer to a paper towel–lined plate to drain. Add the maple syrup and hazelnuts to the butter and stir with a spatula to coat the nuts. Add the balsamic. The sauce will get bubbly at this point.

2. Remove the sauce from the heat (or let reduce slightly if your balsamic wasn't very thick). Stir in the salt and adjust the seasonings as necessary (more salt, or more maple for sweetness). The sauce will thicken quickly, so serve it right away over hot cooked ravioli. Top with the fried sage leaves.

Sweet Potato Gnocchi *with* Bacon, Spinach, *and* Peas

Serves 4

I hope you'll find your own creative ways to use the Sweet Potato Gnocchi (page 216). This is one tasty and easy way that we enjoy the gnocchi at our house, but their uses are limitless.

---

2 to 3 slices peppered bacon, sliced into 1-inch pieces, or one package frozen, sliced bacon (see page 31)

4 cups frozen Sweet Potato Gnocchi (page 216), unthawed (see note)

1 cup frozen peas

2 tablespoons white wine (optional)

½ cup half-and-half

½ cup Chicken Stock (page 202) or vegetable stock

¼ teaspoon salt

2 cups packed baby spinach (see note)

---

1. In a large skillet, cook the bacon over medium heat, rendering the fat and crisping the bacon, 5 to 7 minutes, depending on the thickness of the bacon. Transfer the cooked bacon to a paper towel–lined plate to drain and cool. Drain three quarters of the bacon grease onto paper towels in a paper bag and discard.

2. Let the remaining grease cool slightly, then add the frozen gnocchi (be careful, as the grease might pop a little as you add the cold gnocchi to the pan). Cook without stirring for 3 minutes, or until lightly browned, then flip. Add the peas and cook for 1 minute. Then, add the wine and stir, letting some of it evaporate. Stir in the half-and-half, stock, and salt and bring to a simmer. Add the spinach and stir just until barely wilted. Remove from the heat and serve hot with the bacon on top.

NOTES: *You may also use 1 pound of store-bought potato gnocchi in this dish. Cook according to the package directions, then toss lightly with oil before starting the recipe.*

While we all love this dish, my little boy especially loves it. For him, I chop up the spinach pretty finely.

Thai Noodles *with* Veggies *and* Peanut Sauce

Serves 4

This is a super easy weeknight recipe that is great with frozen ingredients. With the premade and frozen Thai Peanut Sauce (page 208), along with a few cups of frozen veggies, you can have a tasty dinner ready in just 15 minutes. For similar recipes that use frozen ingredients and are made quickly, check out the Orange Sesame Beef Stir-Fry (page 133) and Pork Tacos with Chimichurri and Avocado Slaw (page 123).

8 ounces linguine pasta, broken in half

2 cups vegetable stock

4 cups frozen or fresh vegetables (see note), sliced into preferred sizes

½ cup Thai Peanut Sauce (page 208) (4 to 5 cubes)

½ (15-ounce) can light coconut milk

Thinly sliced fresh basil or chopped fresh cilantro, for garnish

1. Place everything, except the herb garnish, in a large pot. Bring to a boil, then lower the heat to a simmer and cover. Cook for 10 minutes. Season to taste with salt and pepper (I add at least ¼ teaspoon of salt and a few grinds of fresh pepper; see note). Garnish with basil or cilantro and serve.

NOTES: *Consider using the frozen stir-fry veggie bags (see page 24) for this recipe. For more spice, add a few pinches of red pepper flakes. For more peanut butter flavor, add 1 extra tablespoon of straight peanut butter to the mixture.*

Roasted Vegetable-Stuffed Shells

Serves 8 to 10; serve half and freeze half

Right after we had Everett, several friends brought over dinner. I literally had no idea before this moment just how helpful bringing a meal over to a friend could be. We were blessed by every dish brought to our doorstep. My friend Dani brought over her go-to stuffed shells and ever since then I've been playing around with stuffed shells in my own kitchen. This version is loaded with roasted veggies and creamy ricotta cheese.

3 medium-size carrots, chopped into ¼-inch pieces

¼ head of cauliflower, chopped into ¼-inch pieces

1 broccoli crown, chopped into ¼-inch pieces

3 tablespoons olive oil

1¼ teaspoons salt, divided

24 jumbo pasta shells, plus a few more

1 (16-ounce) container ricotta cheese

1 cup shredded mozzarella cheese

½ cup shredded Parmesan cheese

⅛ teaspoon cayenne pepper

1 (26-ounce) jar marinara sauce (3 cups)

1. Preheat the oven to 400°F and line a rimmed baking sheet with foil. Take out one disposable 9 x 13 baking dish or two 9 x 9-square baking dishes.

2. Toss the veggies with the olive oil. Season with 1 teaspoon of the salt and lay flat on the baking sheet. Bake for 25 minutes, or until slightly browned and crispy.

3. Bring a large pot of salted water to a boil. Add the pasta shells (a few more than 24, in case a few break while cooking). Boil for 8 to 10 minutes, or until starting to soften but with a slight bite. (They will cook more when they are baking.)

4. While the pasta is cooking, mix together the three cheeses, the remaining ¼ teaspoon of salt, and the cayenne. Once veggies are done roasting, roughly chop them and add them to the cheese mixture. Pour 1½ cups of the marinara sauce into a rectangular baking dish or into two square baking dishes. Lower the oven temperature to 350°F.

5. Once the pasta is done, drain, reserving ½ cup of the pasta water. Fill each shell with the veggie mixture and place in the baking dish. Mix together the remaining 1½ cups of marinara with the ½ cup of pasta water and pour this over the top of the filled shells.

6. Cover with foil and bake for 20 minutes, then uncover and bake for 5 to 10 more minutes, or until bubbly.

TO FREEZE: *Use the Casserole Method (see page 16) to freeze. When I make this recipe, I like to bake one square dish for dinner and freeze the second one.*

TO BAKE FROM FROZEN: *Preheat oven to 350°F. Remove plastic wrap from the frozen dish, then re-cover with the foil. Place in the preheated oven and bake for 1 hour and 15 minutes, or until bubbling. Remove foil and bake for an additional 10 minutes.*

Fisherman's Stew

Serves 4

I've fallen in love with fish stew time and time again. I first had a cioppino when I was writing a review for a new restaurant. Then, I tasted it again in San Francisco. Then, with the help of my friend Evan, we finally made it at home, even making our own fish broth. My very favorite experience was in Seattle, pier-side, and the stew had just enough sausage to add a perfect amount of spice. This recipe is not meant to be frozen but uses frozen mixed seafood, which makes it super simple to whip up. Make sure you have some crusty bread around when you make this, because the broth is one of the best parts of the dish.

1 tablespoon olive oil

4 ounces chorizo sausage, casings removed

½ yellow onion, diced

2 garlic cloves

1 green bell pepper, seeded and chopped

3 diced tomatoes, or 1 (14-ounce) can diced tomatoes with their juices

¼ cup white wine

1 cup vegetable stock

½ teaspoon salt

⅛ teaspoon freshly ground black pepper

Pinch of red pepper flakes

16 ounces frozen mixed seafood (such as calamari, mussels, shrimp, and white fish)

1 teaspoon fresh basil, chopped

1 teaspoon fresh parsley, chopped

1. Heat a soup pot over medium heat. Heat the oil, then add the sausage and cook until browned, about 8 minutes, using a spoon or spatula to break up the sausage as it cooks.

2. Add the onion and garlic and sauté until translucent, a minute or two. Then add the bell pepper and tomatoes. Use a wooden spoon to scrape any browned bits off the bottom of the pan.

3. Add the white wine and let some evaporate. Continue to use the wooden spoon to stir and scrape along the bottom and sides of the pan.

4. Add the vegetable stock and seasonings and bring to a simmer. Carefully add the frozen seafood to the hot broth. Cook just until the seafood is warmed through, 10 minutes or according to the package directions. (You don't want to overcook the seafood, or it will turn rubbery.) Stir in half of the fresh herbs, then serve the soup with crusty bread and garnish the top with the remaining herbs.

Shrimp *and* Zucchini Spaghetti

Serves 4

I savored every bite of this dish when we visited Italy. One evening we sat on a piazza right next to a tiny harbor opening up to the sea. It was magical. When I asked what was in the dish, the ingredients were too simple not to try at home. The simplicity of the dish, as well as the flavor, make for a magical meal at home or abroad! While this dish uses frozen shrimp, it is not one we freeze after making it. It's quick enough that you can even make it on a weeknight or for a special dinner with friends.

16 to 20 uncooked frozen shrimp

½ pound spaghetti

½ + ⅛ teaspoon salt

2 tablespoons salted butter, divided

2 tablespoons olive oil

4 garlic cloves, minced

1 8-inch zucchini, yielding 1 cup shredded, using a peeler or cheese grater

⅛ teaspoon freshly ground black pepper

1 teaspoon Vegetable Bouillon, page 207 (see note)

¼ cup heavy cream

1. To quickly thaw the shrimp, place them in a colander under cold water for 5 to 7 minutes.

2. Bring a large pot of salted water to a boil. Once the water is boiling, add the pasta and set a timer for 1 minute less than called for in the package directions.

3. While the pasta cooks, dry the thawed shrimp with a paper towel and sprinkle with ⅛ teaspoon of the salt. Heat a large sauté pan over high heat. Add 1 tablespoon of the butter. Once the butter is melted, add the shrimp. Cook for 2 to 3 minutes on each side, or until slightly browned. Once cooked, set aside on a plate.

4. Use a paper towel to carefully wipe out any browning from the hot pan. Place the remaining tablespoon of butter and the oil in the pan and set over medium heat. Add the garlic and cook 30 seconds, then add the zucchini.

5. Once the pasta is done cooking, reserve ½ cup of the cooking liquid, then drain in a colander and rinse with cold water. Add the cooked pasta to the zucchini pan along with remaining ½ teaspoon of salt and the pepper, vegetable bouillon, and reserved pasta water. Pour the cream over the pasta and toss to combine. Transfer to a serving dish and top with the shrimp. Add more salt, if necessary. Serve with crusty bread.

NOTE: *If you haven't made homemade vegetable bouillon yet, use ⅛ teaspoon store-bought vegetable bouillon and add up to ⅛ teaspoon more, if needed. Or just add more salt, to taste.*

DESSERTS

Pie Dough

Makes 2 piecrusts

One summer I was on a quest to figure out pie dough. As it turned out, I just needed more practice making it. I knew all the secrets, such as keeping the butter cold and not overkneading the dough, but I just needed to make more pie in order to make better pie. So, if you're like I was and are not completely confident in your pie-making skills, then get some butter and flour and get to work. I usually make two batches of this dough back to back (make one, then make the other) while I have all the ingredients out, then my freezer is stocked with four pie doughs ready to go, and there are no excuses for me not to make pie when it's berry season or time for potpie in the winter.

---

1 cup (2 sticks, 8 ounces) salted butter, cold

2½ cups all-purpose flour, plus more for dusting

¾ teaspoon salt

2 teaspoons sugar (optional, for sweet pies)

½ to ¾ cup ice-cold water

---

1. Use a cheese grater to grate the cold butter into large pieces or you can slice it into walnut-size pieces. Place the butter back in the fridge.

2. In a large bowl, mix together the flour, salt, and sugar, if using. In a liquid measuring cup, measure out ¾ cup of the ice-cold water . Take the butter out of the fridge and add it to the flour mixture. Use your hands to toss the butter with the flour, coating the cold butter in flour. Then work the butter into the flour until the mixture forms pea-size granules. Don't overmix the butter into the flour or you won't have a flaky crust. Slowly add the water ¼ cup at a time. Work the dough with your hands until it sticks together, adding more cold water as needed. When you can pinch the dough and it stays together, it's ready for the last step.

3. Flour a large cutting board and turn out the dough (with any of the extra flour at the bottom of the bowl) onto the surface. Gently knead just until a ball forms, adding a little cold water if needed (but not too much!). Divide the dough into two equal-size balls, pressing each down to form a disk (disks are just easier to roll out than a ball shape). Wrap each with plastic wrap and place in the refrigerator.

TO FREEZE: You have three options: (1) You can freezing the dough disks, wrapped in plastic and placed in freezer-safe resealable plastic bags; (2) you can roll out the dough and place in disposable pie plates, wrap them tightly with plastic wrap, and freeze this raw dough already formed; or (3) you can roll it out and place in a pie plate, parbake it, let it cool, then freeze it (this is good for fruit pies, quiche, cream pies, or custard pies, such as pumpkin).

TO PARBAKE (OR PREBAKE): First roll out a cold disk of dough and set into a pie plate, then refrigerate for at least 30 minutes. Preheat the oven to 375°F. Line the pie dough with two layers of foil and place pie weights or rice in the lined pie shell, filling it all the way to the top so that the dough stays flat against the pie plate. Place in the hot oven and bake for 20 to 25 minutes, or until the edges start to brown. Remove the pie weights and foil, and bake for an additional 5 to 8 minutes just to finish baking the bottom of the crust. Remove from the oven, let cool, then freeze. Once frozen, wrap tightly with plastic wrap and transfer to a labeled freezer-safe resealable plastic bag.

Vanilla Ice Cream

Makes 1½ quarts

I think everyone should have a go-to recipe for ice cream, along with an ice-cream maker, of course. Once you have mastered this recipe, then you can get as creative as you would like with ice-cream flavors, additions, and toppings. This is my favorite vanilla ice-cream recipe and in fact it's so good that most of the time we don't alter it in any way.

2 cups milk	5 large egg yolks
2 cups heavy cream	Zest of 1 lemon or seeds and
1 cup sugar	pod of 1 vanilla bean (see note)

1. In a medium saucepan, bring the milk, cream, and ½ cup of the sugar to a boil (keep close by, so it doesn't boil over).

2. In a bowl, whisk the egg yolks together with the remaining ½ cup of sugar.

3. Once the milk is boiling, lower the heat to medium-low. Use a measuring cup to transfer about ¼ cup of the hot milk mixture to the egg yolk mixture and quickly whisk to combine. Add another ¼ cup of hot milk mixture to the egg mixture and continue to whisk the two together. Pour the entire egg mixture into the remaining hot milk mixture and add the lemon zest or vanilla bean seeds and pod. Cook, stirring constantly with a wooden spoon and scraping the sides and bottom of the pot, until the custard is thick enough to coat the back of the spoon and leaves a clear trail when a finger is drawn through it on the spoon, about 5 minutes. Do not allow the custard to boil.

4. Pour the custard through a medium-mesh sieve set over a clean bowl. Discard the vanilla bean pod. Cover the custard with plastic wrap (placing the wrap directly against the top of the custard to prevent a skin from forming) and refrigerate until cold, about 1 hour or overnight. Churn with an ice-cream maker for 25 minutes, or according to the manufacturer's directions. Transfer the ice cream to an airtight container and place in the freezer. Freeze for at least 4 hours.

TO FREEZE: For best quality, ice cream lasts 1 month in the freezer. To ensure no ice crystals or freezer burn forms on the top of your ice cream, place parchment or plastic wrap directly against the top surface of the ice cream inside the airtight container you're freezing it in.

NOTE: Whether you use lemon or vanilla depends on how you're going to use this base. For fruitier ice creams I like lemon zest, but for richer ice creams I'll stick with vanilla. If using vanilla, place the vanilla bean on a work surface. Using a small, sharp knife, cut one side of the bean down the center but not all the way through the bean, just enough to open the pod. Using the knife tip or a small spoon, scrape the seeds from the vanilla bean. Alternatively, you can use 1 teaspoon of pure vanilla extract instead of the vanilla bean seeds.

Basic Yellow Cake

Makes 1 two-layer 8- or 9-inch cake, or 1 single-layer 9 x 13-inch cake

As with a good vanilla ice-cream recipe, everyone needs a basic yellow cake recipe for birthdays or other celebrations. This one can even be made on the fly, since it doesn't require cake flour. I love making an ice-cream cake with this recipe, but the cake also good with a whipped chocolate frosting. Freeze it right after it cools and then it will be perfectly moist when it defrosts.

¾ cup (1½ sticks, 6 ounces) salted butter, at room temperature (see note)

1½ cups sugar

3 large eggs, at room temperature (see note)

2½ cups all-purpose flour

2½ teaspoons baking powder

½ teaspoon salt

1¼ cups milk

2 teaspoons pure vanilla extract

---

1. Preheat the oven to 375°F. Grease two 8- or 9-inch round cake pans or one 9 x 13-inch rectangular cake pan with baking spray and line the bottom of each pan with a circle of parchment paper. Spray the parchment paper as well.

2. In a stand mixer fitted with a whisk attachment, combine the butter and sugar. Whip until light and fluffy. Add one egg at a time, scraping down the sides and bottom of the bowl with a spatula between additions. In a medium-size bowl, mix together the dry ingredients. Add the dry ingredients to the wet mixture, alternating with the milk, in three additions. Stir in the vanilla.

3. Pour the batter into the prepared pans and set on the middle rack of the oven. Bake the 8-inch cakes for 30 to 35 minutes, or until the cake bounces back when you press down lightly on its surface with a finger. Baking times for other cake pans: 9-inch: 20 to 25 minutes; 9 x 13-inch: 15 to 30 minutes.

4. Remove from the oven and let rest in the pans for 5 minutes before inverting them onto a wire cooling rack. Let cool completely before freezing or filling with ice cream.

TO FREEZE: Use the Wrap and Bag Method (see page 16) to freeze.

NOTE: To quickly bring butter to room temperature, microwave in 5-second bursts on high for up to 15 seconds total, or until starting to soften but not melt. And to get eggs to room temperature, place them in a small bowl of warm water.

Sea Salt Chocolate Chip Cookies

Makes 18 extra-large or 24 to 30 small cookies

Having cookie dough ready to go in your freezer is perfect if you like to host on the fly. I like to form the dough for this cookie into a log before freezing, so that I can slice a few and bake at any moment. Late-night TV-watching desserts or post-naptime treats are suddenly brought to a new level.

1¼ cups (2½ sticks, 10 ounces) salted butter, at room temperature (see note)

1½ cups packed light brown sugar

1 cup granulated sugar

2 large eggs, at room temperature (see note)

2 teaspoons vanilla extract

3½ cups all-purpose flour

2 teaspoons baking powder

¼ teaspoon sea salt, plus more for sprinkling

2 cups bittersweet chocolate chips (12 ounces)

TO FREEZE: *Lay out a large piece of plastic wrap. Scoop half of the dough onto the plastic wrap and form a log. Wrap the dough tightly, then twist the ends of the wrap or tie with kitchen string. Repeat with the second half of the dough. Freeze, then store the wrapped dough in a freezer-safe resealable plastic bag.*

For best quality, the cookie dough lasts 3 months in the freezer. Label with the baking temperature and time. Slice and bake this dough straight from the freezer.

TO BAKE FROM FROZEN DOUGH: *Preheat the oven to 375°F and slice the logs into ¾- to 1-inch-thick rounds (however many you'd like to bake), then place on a parchment-lined baking sheet, leaving 2 inches between cookies. I like to squeeze the slices slightly into a ball before placing them in the oven, so the cookies bake a little taller. Sprinkle with sea salt, then into the oven they go! Bake for 14 to 16 minutes depending on size of cookies, or until golden brown on the edge and slightly more pale in the center.*

NOTE: *To quickly bring butter to room temperature, microwave in 5-second bursts on high for up to 15 seconds, or until starting to soften but not melt. And to get eggs to room temperature, place them in a small bowl of warm water.*

1. In a large stand mixer fitted with the paddle attachment, cream together the butter and both sugars. Once light and fluffy, add the eggs one at a time, scraping down the sides of the bowl with a spatula between additions. Beat in the vanilla. In a separate bowl, mix together the flour, baking powder, and sea salt. Stop the mixer and add the entire flour mixture to the wet ingredients. Pulse the mixer on and off to mix the flour into the dough just until incorporated; do not overmix. Stir in the chocolate chips.

2. If baking some of the dough and not freezing it, refrigerate for 20 to 30 minutes before baking, and preheat the oven to 350°F. Use an ice-cream scoop for large cookies or a tablespoon for smaller to divide the dough onto a parchment-lined baking sheet, leaving 2 inches between cookies. Sprinkle with coarse sea salt. Bake for 12 to 14 minutes depending on size of cookies, or until golden brown on the edge and slightly paler in the center (it may take less time for smaller cookies).

Butterscotch Oatmeal Cookies

Makes 2 dozen cookies

My friend Haley and I first made these together and I found butterscotch to be the perfect partner to an old favorite, the oatmeal cookie. These cookies are great on their own, but they also make great ice-cream sandwiches. Use a cookie scoop or tablespoon to make the perfect size of dough ball, then freeze. When baked from frozen, these cookies don't spread out too much but keep a small, round cookie form.

---

3 cups old-fashioned rolled oats

1½ cups all-purpose flour

1 teaspoon baking soda

½ teaspoon salt

¾ cup dark brown sugar

½ cup granulated sugar

1 cup (2 sticks, 8 ounces) butter, room temperature (see note)

2 eggs, at room temperature (see note)

2 teaspoons pure vanilla extract

1 cup butterscotch chips

---

1. Line a baking sheet with parchment paper.

2. Combine the oats, flour, baking soda, and salt in a medium-size bowl. In a stand mixer fitted with the paddle attachment or in a bowl and using a hand mixer, cream together the sugars with the butter until light and fluffy. Add the eggs one at a time, scraping down the sides of the bowl with a spatula between additions. Beat in the vanilla, then mix in the flour mixture just until incorporated; do not overmix. Stir in the butterscotch chips.

3. Scoop the dough onto the prepared baking sheet and bake or freeze.

4. Bake in a preheated 350°F oven for 10 to 12 minutes, leaving 2 inches between cookies, rotating the pan after 8 minutes.

TO FREEZE: Lay Out and Freeze (page 14) by using a cookie scoop or tablespoon to spoon the dough out onto a parchment-lined baking sheet and place in the freezer (you don't need to space them out very far since you're not baking them yet). Once frozen, transfer the pre-scooped dough to a freezer-safe plastic bag. Alternatively, you can roll the dough into a log as described with the Sea Salt Chocolate Chip Cookies (page 172). Label the bag with baking temperature and time.

TO BAKE FROM FROZEN: Place on a parchment-lined baking sheet, leaving 2 inches between cookies, and bake in a preheated 350°F oven for 15 minutes, rotating the pan after 8 minutes.

NOTE: To quickly bring butter to room temperature, microwave in 5-second bursts on high for up to 15 seconds, or until starting to soften but not melt. And to get eggs to room temperature, place them in a small bowl of warm water.

Cereal Milk Ice Cream

Makes 1½ quarts

I first had cereal milk ice cream when some new friends had us over for a nice dinner. Years later I visited New York and had the famous cereal milk soft-serve there. Both experiences had me nostalgic about childhood cereals. So, when I created this recipe I had to use one of my childhood favorites—Cap'n Crunch—but feel free to play around with some of yours.

1 recipe Vanilla Ice Cream (page 168), using half of the sugar (½ cup only) and no lemon zest or vanilla bean

½ teaspoon salt

2 cups Cap'n Crunch cereal (or cereal of your choice)

1. Cook the ice-cream custard with the salt according to the directions on page 168, but do not freeze it. Place the cereal in a heatproof bowl and pour the warm custard over the cereal. Let sit for 20 minutes, while the custard is cooling.

2. Pour the custard mixture through a medium-mesh sieve into a clean bowl. Discard the cereal. Cover the top of the custard with plastic wrap (the wrap should be in direct contact with the top of the custard to prevent any skin from forming). Refrigerate until cold, about 1 hour, or overnight. Then, churn with an ice-cream maker, about 25 minutes or according to the manufacturer's directions.

3. Transfer to a rigid freezer container and freeze for at least 4 hours before serving.

Ice Cream Cake

Makes 1 two-layer 8-inch cake

This fun and quirky dessert brings on a party all on its own. You'll want to bust out the colorful cereals to top the cake (I'm sure you'll have no problem getting rid of the rest of the box!). Use a baked but unfrozen cake and slightly thawed or freshly churned ice cream. I like to make the cake the day before, then wrap it tightly in plastic wrap and refrigerate it, so it doesn't dry out. The ice cream can be made a few days in advance as well.

1 recipe Basic Yellow Cake (page 172), baked in 2 (8-inch) rounds and refrigerated but not frozen

1 quart Cereal Milk Ice Cream (page 177)
Dry cereal, for topping

1. If the ice cream is frozen solid, set it out on the counter to defrost just slightly so it's spreadable for the layers. Unwrap the two layers of yellow cake and set out both on a cutting board. Slice just ⅛ to ¼ inch off the top of both cakes (reserving the removed cake). Spread 1½ to 2 cups of ice cream over one of the cake rounds. Top with the second cake, then spread another 1½ to 2 cups of ice cream over the top of the cake. Sprinkle with the cereal and place in an 8-inch round cake pan (a springform pan works best). Place in the freezer until firm, about 4 hours or overnight. Once frozen, remove from the cake pan and wrap tightly with plastic wrap, then bag or double wrap.

2. **To serve:** Set the frozen cake on a cake stand or cutting board to defrost slightly, 15 to 20 minutes, then use a sharp knife to cut slices. Serve with extra cereal.

NO-WASTE TIP: Save the excess cake and freeze for later use with Wrap and Bag Method (page 16). You can make use of the extra cake for smaller cake and ice cream parfaits layered in jars or to crumble on top of ice cream.

TIP: Dip your knife into hot water before slicing the cake.

Salted Caramel Brownies on a Stick

Makes 10 to 12 brownies

You can use your favorite brownie recipe or a store-bought brownie mix; just make sure to let the brownies cool and harden a little in the fridge before cutting them. I'm including my favorite brownie recipe because it's great just by itself, and if you don't already have a favorite maybe this will become yours, too. My brownies form a crust on top, which you can remove for the brownies on a stick or just press it down so that the surface is even for dipping into chocolate.

BROWNIES

10 tablespoons (5 ounces) salted butter

1 cup semisweet chocolate (5 ounces)

1½ teaspoons pure vanilla extract

4 large eggs

2 cups granulated sugar

½ teaspoon salt

1 cup all-purpose flour

CHOCOLATE COATING

2 cups semisweet chocolate (about 10 ounces)

4 teaspoons vegetable shortening

SALTED CARAMEL

¼ cup (½ stick, 2 ounces) butter

¼ cup light brown sugar

¼ cup heavy cream

¼ teaspoon sea salt, plus more for sprinkling on top

1. **Make the brownies:** Preheat the oven to 400°F and line a 9-inch square baking pan with parchment, then spray the parchment with nonstick cooking spray.

2. Melt the butter and chocolate in a small saucepan over medium-low heat, stirring constantly with a spatula. Once melted, stir in the vanilla and set aside. In a stand mixer fitted with the whisk attachment, whip the eggs, granulated sugar, and salt until pale and light, 8 minutes (I usually set a timer for this step). Slowly pour the warm chocolate mixture into the whipped eggs with the mixer on the lowest setting. Sprinkle the flour over the mixture and stir to combine.

3. Pour the batter into the prepared baking pan and bake for 45 minutes. Remove from the oven and let cool completely, then use edges of parchment to lift the brownies out of the pan. Place the brownies in the fridge to harden a little more before cutting into squares or rectangles. Once totally cool and slightly hard, place on a cutting board and use a sharp knife

to cut the brownies into your desired shapes. Insert a Popsicle stick into each brownie.

4. **Make the chocolate coating:** Melt the chocolate with the shortening in a saucepan over low heat, stirring continuously, or in the microwave on high, stirring every 10 seconds. Pour the chocolate mixture into a wide cup or small bowl. Holding them by their Popsicle stick, dip the brownies into the chocolate and set on a parchment-lined baking sheet to cool and dry. If the chocolate starts to harden or thicken as you're dipping, reheat it briefly on the stovetop in the microwave for 5 to 10 seconds.

5. **Make the salted caramel:** Place all the caramel ingredients in a small saucepan and melt over low heat, stirring to prevent the sugar from burning. Once melted and combined, raise the heat to high and bring to a boil. Once boiling, lower the heat to medium-high and boil for 3 minutes. Remove from the heat. Use a fork or a small wire whisk to fan the caramel onto the brownies. Sprinkle the finished brownies with sea salt. Reserve any leftover caramel and chocolate for ice-cream toppings, rewarming the chocolate as needed.

6. **To serve:** Let brownies thaw for at least 10 to 15 minutes before serving, or you can bring these with you to a picnic or gathering and they'll be ready by the time you arrive.

TO FREEZE: Use the Lay Out and Freeze Method (see page 14) to freeze the brownies.

Blueberry Pie Ice Cream

Makes 1½ quarts

I'm not a big fruity ice cream kind of person and will happily turn down sorbets or sherbets, but even though there is fruit in this treat, it is my favorite ice-cream creation yet. This is a rich custard swirled with sweetened blueberries and crunchy grahams. How could you not love the combo of pie and ice cream in one scoop?!

BLUEBERRY ICE CREAM

1 recipe Vanilla Ice Cream (page 168), using lemon zest (see note)

2 cups blueberries

¼ cup sugar

Pinch of salt

GRAHAM CRACKER CRUMBLE

8 ounces graham crackers (about 14 full crackers)

5 tablespoons salted butter, melted

2 tablespoons all-purpose flour

1. **Start making the blueberry ice cream:** Cook the ice cream according to the directions on page 168 but do not churn or freeze; instead, place it in the refrigerator to cool. Combine the blueberries, sugar, and salt in a small saucepan over medium heat. Simmer until thickened, stirring occasionally, about 1 hour. While the blueberries are cooking, start churning the ice cream in your ice-cream machine.

2. **Make the graham cracker crumble:** Preheat the oven to 350°F and line a sheet pan with parchment paper. In a food processor, pulse half of the crackers to a fine crumb. Add the other half and pulse just a few times, letting some larger pieces remain. Remove the bowl from the processor and stir in the melted butter and flour, using your hands to combine as necessary. Spread this mixture on the prepared sheet pan in an even layer and bake for 10 minutes, then remove from the oven and let cool.

3. **To assemble:** In a quart-size rigid plastic freezer container, layer about one quarter each of the churned vanilla ice cream, then the blueberries, then the graham cracker crumble. Continue layering three to four times. You will probably have leftover blueberry sauce and graham cracker crumble, but I trust you'll find ways to use it (top your oatmeal, yogurt, etc.)!

4. Freeze the ice cream for at least 4 hours. Serve with extra graham cracker crumble.

NOTE: You may use store-bought vanilla ice cream in a pinch. Let it defrost slightly so that you can stir in or layer the blueberries and graham cracker crumble.

Lemon Cream Bars

Makes 9 bars

This recipe is inspired by a dessert we made for our culinary school graduation. Making it does entail a few steps, but nothing too hard. Make sure to read through the directions first and get out everything you need before starting. I promise the end result is worth the work that this takes! When tasted against a chocolate dessert, even chocolate lovers picked this!

CRUST

10 to 12 honey graham crackers

¼ cup (½ stick, 2 ounces) salted butter, melted

⅛ teaspoon salt

CREAM

8 ounces heavy cream

2 tablespoons sugar

Zest of ½ lemon

LEMON FILLING

¾ cup freshly squeezed lemon juice (3 to 4 lemons)

1 cup sugar

½ cup (1 stick, 4 ounces) butter

½ teaspoon salt

4 large eggs

4 large egg yolks

1 (1½-teaspoon) packet unflavored gelatin

1. **Make the crust:** Preheat the oven to 350°F. Use a food processor or blender to reduce the graham crackers to fine crumbs. In a medium-size bowl, mix 1½ cups of the crumbs with the melted butter and salt. Transfer the mixture to a 9-inch square baking pan and use your hands to firmly press the crumbs down. Bake the crust for 8 minutes.

2. **Make the cream:** In a large mixing bowl, using a stand mixer or handheld with a whisk attachment, whip the cream until soft peaks form. Add the sugar and lemon zest and continue to whip for 30 more seconds. Transfer to a smaller bowl and place in the fridge.

3. **Make the lemon filling:** Set a wire sieve over a bowl. Place a double boiler, with water in the bottom pan, over high heat. Heat the lemon juice, sugar, butter, and salt in the top of the double boiler, stirring often, until really hot but not boiling.

4. While the juice mixture is heating up, whisk together the eggs and egg yolks in a separate bowl. Once the juice mixture is hot, transfer ¼ cup of it to the egg mixture and quickly whisk the two together. Do this once more with another

¼ cup of hot juice mixture, then pour the entire egg mixture into the remaining hot juice mixture. Use a wire whisk to quickly mix the eggs into the hot mixture for 2 to 5 minutes, or until thickened, stirring constantly to prevent the eggs from scrambling and the sauce from sticking. Once thick (test by coating the back of a spoon with the filling and swiping your finger down the spoon; if it leaves a clear trail, it is thick enough), pour through the wire sieve, using a spatula to press the liquid through quickly. Sprinkle the gelatin over the hot filling, then quickly mix it all together to incorporate and break apart any clumps of gelatin.

5. Pour the lemon filling over the crust. Place the pan in the fridge to cool for 30 minutes. Once the filling is cool and set, spread the whipped cream over the top.

TO FREEZE: Place the uncovered bars that have been topped with whipped cream in the freezer. Once frozen, use the Casserole Method (see page 16) to freeze. These can also be cut and wrapped separately for individual treats.

To serve, let sit on the counter for 5 to 10 minutes, then cut and serve.

TIP: Dip your knife into hot water before slicing up the bars.

Brown Sugar Peach Pie

Makes 1 pie

Using frozen peach pie filling and frozen pie dough, I like to freeze the filling in a pie plate, so it holds the right shape and is ready to be placed in a crust and baked. Once you've made this, you're one step away from homemade pie. This is also great for apple pie, or any mixture of berry or cherry pie. Be sure to start to thaw the piecrust overnight in the refrigerator the night before you plan to bake it.

PEACH PIE FILLING

7 large peaches

¼ to ⅓ cup all-purpose flour, depending on the juiciness of your peaches

½ cup light brown sugar

½ teaspoon ground cinnamon

½ teaspoon grated fresh ginger (see note)

¼ teaspoon salt

PIECRUST

½ recipe Pie Dough (page 167), pre-baked and frozen

All-purpose flour, for dusting

BROWN SUGAR STREUSEL TOPPING

1 cup all-purpose flour

3 tablespoons packed light brown sugar

2 tablespoons granulated sugar

¼ teaspoon salt

6 tablespoons unsalted butter, cut into ½-inch cubes, at room temperature

1. **Make the peach filling:** Slice the peaches into relatively uniform slices (about 12 per peach). I like to keep the skin on, one less step in the recipe, but if you prefer not to have the skin, then remove it before slicing (see note). Gently toss the sliced peaches with all the other ingredients.

2. Line a pie plate with two long pieces of plastic wrap crisscrossed one over the other. Spoon the filling into the prepared pie plate. It should be slightly mounded on top because the peaches will shrink down as they cook. Wrap the pile of peaches with the long edges of plastic wrap and place the whole pie plate in the freezer.

3. Once frozen, transfer the wrapped filling to a freezer-safe resealable plastic bag (see the Wrap and Bag Method, page 16).

4. **Assemble and bake the pie:** Set the frozen piecrust in the refrigerator overnight to thaw. If you have a pre-baked frozen pie shell, use that, but if not you'll want to pre-bake your crust before filling it. Roll out the dough on a floured surface, adding more flour as needed so the dough doesn't stick to the surface. Flip and rotate the dough as you're rolling it out. Place the rolled-out piecrust in a pie plate and set it back into the refrigerator while you prepare the streusel topping. If you still need to pre-bake your crust, get the rolled-out dough out of the fridge and cover with two layers of foil, just over the top of the pie. Add dried beans, rice, or pie weights on top of the foil. Pre-bake for 12 to 15 minutes at 425°F or 20 to 25 minutes at 375°F. Carefully remove pie weights and uncover the foil. Place back in the oven for 5 to 10 minutes to finish cooking the bottom of the crust.

5. **Make the streusel topping:** In a medium-size bowl, mix together all the streusel ingredients. Set aside.

6. Once cooked, let the pie rest for 10 minutes, then place the frozen peach pie filling inside the crust, and top with streusel mixture.

7. Bake on the middle rack of the oven at 425°F with a rimmed baking sheet on a rack below. Bake for 25 minutes, then lower the temperature to 375°F, and bake for an additional 45 to 60 minutes or until bubbly with a brown crust and crisp streusel. Cover the edges of the crust with a donut-shaped piece of foil if the edges start to brown.

8. Remove from the oven and let cool for at least 30 minutes, or up to 2 hours before serving.

NOTES: If you desire peeled peaches for your pie, see page 23 for directions to peel. For directions on freezing fresh ginger, see page 28.

Fruit and Yogurt Pops

Makes 6 to 8 pops

These pops are the perfect afternoon treat on a hot summer day. When we make them, we like to use an assortment of fruits so that we have a variety of flavors to choose from.

1½ cups vanilla yogurt
   (not Greek yogurt)
½ cup sugar
½ cup water

2 cups fruit, either mixed or one kind
   (fresh fruit is easier to blend than
   frozen for this recipe)
½ cup granola, for serving (page 46)

1. In a small saucepan over medium heat, dissolve the sugar in the water to make a simple syrup. Once dissolved, set the syrup aside to cool. If using a few different kinds of fruit, set them out in separate bowls. In a high-powered blender, blend ¼ cup of fruit with 1 to 2 tablespoons of simple syrup, depending on how sweet you'd like these. Repeat with remaining fruit or blend all the fruit with ½ to ¾ cup of simple syrup. In a Popsicle mold, layer the yogurt, fruit, yogurt, fruit, yogurt.

2. Place in the freezer to freeze. Once frozen, transfer to a large freezer-safe resealable plastic bag to store. When ready to serve, you can dip the pops into granola. Save any leftover simple syrup for cocktails.

TO FREEZE: Use the Lay Out and Freeze Method (page 14), then bag.

Grape Slushy

Serves 4

How does anyone keep grapes in their home for longer than a couple of days? I know my family, including myself, eat them mindlessly, then we all wonder how they disappeared. Next time you see grapes on sale, buy two bags and freeze one of the bags. Not only are frozen grapes a great snack, but kids and adults alike love this grape slushy recipe. For a grown-up version, add gin for a slushy cocktail and top with mint. Make sure to blend the grapes well or you might get some grape skins in the mixture.

---

3 cups frozen grapes (see page 23)   1½ to 2 cups coconut water, or enough to cover the grapes

---

1. Place the grapes in the food processor, then add enough coconut water to cover them. Blend until smooth and the grape skins should be pretty fine. Serve immediately.

Blueberry Butterscotch Ice Cream Sandwiches

Makes 6 ice-cream sandwiches

Putting my favorite ice cream between two chewy cookies . . . well, it just doesn't get much better than that! For this fun combo, I use the Butterscotch Oatmeal Cookies (page 174) along with Blueberry Pie Ice Cream (page 183). If you already have both on hand, this dessert is a cinch to put together, but if you only have one of the two, feel free to substitute store-bought ice cream or oatmeal cookies.

12 Butterscotch Oatmeal Cookies (page 174)

2 cups Blueberry Pie Ice Cream (page 183)

1. Bake the oatmeal cookies and let cool on a wire rack.

2. Set out 2 cups of blueberry pie ice cream to thaw slightly, 5 minutes.

3. Lay out six cookies, face down. Use a small cookie scoop to place about ¼ cup of the ice cream on each cookie. Top the ice cream with the remaining six cookies and gently squeeze the cookie pairs together so the ice cream comes out to the edge. Use a clean index finger to swipe around the ice cream for an even edge.

TO FREEZE: Use the Lay Out and Freeze Method (see page 14) to freeze.

Coffee Granita

Makes 3 cups granita

My husband is a part owner of a thriving local coffee business. I couldn't write a book without including something coffee related. Over the summer he created a super-refreshing cold-brew that we now sell by the bottle. I created this recipe based on using two bottles of cold-brew, then just adding the sugar. If you can't find cold-brew coffee at your local grocery store, you can make cold brew at home or just brew your favorite strong coffee and let it cool.

3 cups cold-brew coffee or cooled strong coffee (see note)

¾ cup sugar

1 teaspoon pure vanilla extract

1. Combine the coffee and sugar in a pot over medium heat. Simmer until all the sugar is dissolved. Remove from the heat and stir in the vanilla. Let cool, then pour into a 9 x 13-inch pan. Place the pan in the freezer and set a timer for 1 hour.

2. After an hour, use a fork to rake the mixture and break up the ice crystals. Continue to freeze, and every 30 minutes, rake the mixture until it is completely frozen and granular throughout (3 to 4 hours total). Serve with whipped cream or Vanilla Ice Cream (page 168).

TO FREEZE: *Use the Casserole Method (see page 16) to freeze until ready to serve.*

NOTE: *Use 4 cups of water and ½ cup of ground coffee to prepare strong coffee.*

BEYOND BASICS

Any Nut Pesto

Makes 2½ cups pesto

One thing I can't seem to kill in my garden is herbs. Every year I grow a ton of them! I found many ways to store them for winter (see page 28), but pesto is my all-time favorite for using fresh basil. This recipe can be made with any nut, though I have found that walnuts, pine nuts, and hazelnuts are my favorites.

---

1 cup nuts (see note)
4 cups tightly packed fresh basil
4 garlic cloves, skin removed
1 cup olive oil

1 cup shredded or grated Parmesan cheese
1 teaspoon salt
⅛ teaspoon freshly ground black pepper

---

1. Preheat the oven to 375°F. Lay out the nuts in a single layer (not overlapping)on an ungreased rimmed baking sheet. Toast for 8 to 10 minutes, or until fragrant (use less time for smaller nuts, such as pine nuts). Remove from the oven and let cool, then use your fingertips to rub any loose skin off the nuts.

2. Using a food processor or high-powered blender, pulse the basil and cooled nuts until all the leaves are processed. Add the garlic and oil and process until the mixture resembles a coarse paste. Add the Parmesan and seasoning. Pulse just until combined. Taste and adjust the seasoning, if necessary.

TO FREEZE: Use the Ice Cube Method (see page 16) or Divide and Portion Method (see page 15) to freeze in freezer-safe resealable plastic bags or five 4-ounce freezer-safe jars.
    The pesto lasts 6 months in the freezer.

NOTE: Lightly colored nuts, such as cashews or pine nuts, make for a brighter green pesto. To prevent your pesto from browning quickly (oxidizing) you can quickly blanch the basil first, then cool in an ice-water bath (fill one large bowl with ice water and place the basil in another bowl on top) and let dry before processing, or you can add a tablespoon or so of freshly squeezed lemon juice.

Classic Tomato Sauce

Makes 16 cups sauce

I started making homemade tomato sauce a few years back and haven't looked back since. At the end of the summer I get a box of ripe local tomatoes and reserve an afternoon or evening for this project. Usually we can make it through the whole winter without buying tomato sauce from the store.

---

12 pounds Roma tomatoes

¼ cup + 2 tablespoons olive oil, divided

2 onions, diced

5 garlic cloves, finely diced

3 carrots, sliced into ¼-inch rounds

3 celery stalks, sliced into ¼-inch pieces

1 cup red wine

¼ cup chopped fresh oregano, or 4 sprigs

¼ cup chopped fresh basil, or 4 sprigs

1 teaspoon salt

¼ teaspoon freshly ground black pepper

---

1. **To peel the tomatoes:** Heat a large pot of water to a boil and set out a large bowl of ice-cold water. Use a paring knife to score an X on the bottom of every tomato, being careful not to slice too deeply as the tomato will cook in the water (which you don't want). Carefully place tomatoes in boiling water for 30 seconds to 1 minute (depending on the ripeness of the tomato). The tomato is ready when the skin starts to peel away at the X. Use a slotted spoon to transfer tomatoes into the cool water bath. Once they are cool enough to touch, start peeling.

2. Once peeled, quarter the tomatoes and remove the cores and seeds. I place a large wire sieve over a bowl near my cutting board and scoop the seeds and juices into it. Once you're done seeding the tomatoes, use your hands to press the seeds and juices against the wire sieve so only the juices go into the bowl underneath. Then you can use all the juices and nothing goes to waste. When I am done, I get around 4 cups of juice. Discard just the cores and seeds.

3. Heat a large pot over medium-high heat. Heat the ¼ cup of olive oil and add the onions and garlic. Sauté for 3 minutes, or until the onions become translucent. Add the carrots and celery and continue to cook for 5 to 10 minutes. Pour in the red wine and stir, letting some of the alcohol evaporate. Add all the tomatoes and their juices. Add the herbs (if you keep

them on their stems, you can just remove the whole stem
after cooking the sauce). Simmer the sauce for 1 hour. Use an
immersion blender to blend until smooth, or let cool over an
ice-water bath (fill one large bowl with ice water and place the
sauce in another bowl on top), then blend in batches in a high-
powered blender. Add the remaining 2 tablespoons of olive oil
to the finished sauce and season to taste with salt and pepper.

TO FREEZE: *Use the Divide and Portion
Method (see page 15) to freeze.*

Super Simple Chicken Stock 2 Ways

Yields 2½ quarts

Everyone should be making their own stock at home. You can make it easily in two different ways, either with a whole chicken (meat on)—then you can use the cooked meat in soups, enchiladas, and so on; or using the carcass of a roasted or rotisserie chicken. Both ways are almost effortless. All it takes is a little time. And if you don't have the time, you can also freeze meatless chicken bones and make the stock when you do have a little extra time.

---

1 whole raw chicken or the carcass (bones) of 1 roasted or rotisserie chicken	2 celery stalks
	3 parsley sprigs
	3 thyme sprigs
4 quarts water	1 teaspoon whole black peppercorns
1 large yellow onion, chopped	1 teaspoon salt (use ½ teaspoon if using
2 carrots	a rotisserie chicken)

TO FREEZE THE MEAT FROM A COOKED CHICKEN: *It is easiest to remove chicken meat from the bones when it is still warm. Wait until it is just cool enough to handle, then remove the meat. Remove all the meat from the whole chicken, even from the back of the chicken. Use the Divide and Portion Method (see page 15) to transfer by 1 to 2 cupfuls into vacuum-seal bags and seal. Label and freeze.*

TO FREEZE THE STOCK: *Use the Divide and Portion Method (see page 16). I like to use quart-size rigid-sided plastic containers for stocks or to freeze some in muffin tins for when I need a small amount of stock in a recipe. You can freeze right away or refrigerate overnight, then skim the fat off the top of the stock before freezing. You can also remove the fat and simmer the stock down further, concentrating it so that it doesn't take as much storage space.*

NOTE: *Ever wonder what those grayish bubbles are on the top of your broth? These are just impurities in the broth. For the purest consommé, use a spoon to skim this off while the broth is cooking.*

1. If using a roasted or rotisserie chicken, remove all the meat and reserve for a meal or to freeze. In a stockpot, bring the water, whole chicken or carcass, all the vegetables, and the seasonings to a boil, then lower the heat to a simmer and cook for 1½ hours, skimming off any gray bubbles (see note) from the top of the stock. Prepare an ice-water bath by setting one bowl on top of a slightly larger bowl filled with ice. Take a third bowl (with a pour spout, if you have one) and set a colander over it. Strain the stock through the colander into the bowl. Discard all the solid veggies and bones (if you used a whole chicken, remove the meat and set aside to freeze). Strain the stock a second time through a fine wire-mesh strainer and into the top bowl of the ice bath.

Beef Stock and Bone Broth

Yields 3½ quarts

There is a whole craze about bone broth right now. At first I was confused, but as I started to look into it, I found that just a few simple steps differentiate a stock from a bone broth: If you want to make a bone broth, add some cider vinegar to draw out the marrow and gelatin (which is what is most nutritious) from the bones, then simmer the broth for over 10 hours. If you desire a simpler beef stock, you just need 2½ hours to simmer the stock. Both have healthy benefits; one is just more enhanced than the other.

1 teaspoon olive oil	½ cup red wine
3 pounds veal bones (see note)	½ cup water
2 ounces tomato paste	1 tablespoon cider vinegar (see note)
1 onion, chopped into large pieces	1 thyme sprig
3 carrots, peeled and sliced into 1-inch pieces	2 to 3 parsley sprigs
3 celery stalks, washed and sliced into 1-inch pieces	1 bay leaf
	1 teaspoon black peppercorns
	1 teaspoon salt

1. Preheat the oven to 400°F and lightly grease a rimmed baking sheet with the oil. Place all the bones on the baking sheet. Roast for 30 minutes.

2. Remove the pan from the oven and use the back of a spoon to paint the tomato paste onto the bones. Add the onion, carrots, and celery to the baking sheet in a single layer, not overlapping. Place the tomato-covered bones along with the veggies back into the oven for 20 more minutes.

3. Transfer the bones and veggies to a separate bowl. Place the baking sheet over two burners on the stovetop. Add the wine and water to the pan over medium heat. Deglaze the pan, using a wooden spoon to scrape off the browned bits on the pan. Reserve this liquid.

4. Once the bones are cool, place a large stockpot on the stovetop over medium-high heat. Add the bones, veggies, and wine mixture, along with the cider vinegar (if you are making bone broth). Add 6 quarts of cold water to the pot along with all the herbs and seasonings. Bring to a boil, then lower the heat to a

(continued)

low simmer. Cook for at least 2½ hours. (The longer you cook the broth, the more savory and nutritious it will become. If you lower the heat to the lowest simmer, you may continue to cook the broth for 12 to 24 hours, or even place in a 200°F oven for the same amount of time or into a slow cooker on LOW.) While simmering, occasionally skim fat and foam from the top, using a ladle. The stock is ready when a carrot can be easily mashed (remove the carrot from the pot and use the back of a spoon to test the carrot). Strain through a colander into a large bowl or pot, then again through a fine-mesh strainer. Cool over an ice-water bath (fill one large bowl with ice water and place the broth in another bowl on top).

TO FREEZE: *Use the Divide and Portion Method (see page 15) or Ice Cube Method (page 16) to freeze. I like to use quart-size rigid plastic containers for stocks, or to freeze some in muffin tins for when I need a small amount of stock in a recipe. You can freeze right away or refrigerate overnight, then skim the fat off the top of the broth before freezing. You can also remove the fat and simmer the stock down further, concentrating it so that it doesn't take as much storage space.*

NOTES: *If you desire to skip the step of roasting the bones and veggies before making the broth, you can make a beef broth in the same way as described with the chicken stock.*
   Cider vinegar helps extract the nutrients from the bones.

Vegetable Bouillon

Makes about 3 cups bouillon concentrate

1 teaspoon bouillon per 1 cup water, adjusting to your preferences

After making this the first time, I couldn't stop telling people about it! How had I not thought of this before?! The wonderful thing about this is not only that you always have a supply of stock on hand, but also the fact that it takes up hardly any space in the freezer or fridge. I keep a small jar in my fridge for quick use and the rest of the batch goes into the freezer. Because of its salt content, it won't freeze solid and you can also use it immediately while frozen. Make sure you wash and trim all your veggies well before puréeing them.

1 cup + 1 teaspoon water

⅓ cup Slow-Roasted Tomatoes (page 209) or sun-dried tomatoes (10 to 12 tomatoes)

1 large shallot, peeled and sliced

3 medium-size garlic cloves, peeled and sliced

2 celery stalks, sliced into ½-inch pieces

2 medium leeks, white parts only, rinsed well and sliced

5 medium carrots, peeled and sliced into ½-inch pieces

¼ cup salt (see note)

1 teaspoon black peppercorns

1 tablespoon fresh thyme

½ small bundle fresh parsley, including stems, rinsed and dried

1. Place all the ingredients (see note) in the large bowl of a food processor (should hold 8 cups or more). If you have a smaller food processor you can process in batches, as the ingredients will collapse as you grind them up, making room for more.

TO FREEZE: *Use the Divide and Portion Method (page 15) to freeze into freezer-safe jars or resealable plastic bags. The bouillon won't completely solidify in the freezer because of the salt content, so you can just take spoonfuls straight out of the freezer to mix with water.*

NOTES: *The salt cures the vegetables and inhibits bacteria growth in bouillon. Also, keep in mind that this is a concentrate. However, since you are freezing this bouillon, you can skip the salt altogether or alter the amount to your liking and adjust the salt later as you're cooking. If you want to store this in your refrigerator, you need to double the salt to 6 ounces for appropriate curing.*

To store in the fridge, let the bouillon cure for 1 week before using. The bouillon mixture will keep in the fridge for 3 months or frozen for 6 months.

Thai Peanut Sauce

Makes 3 cups

Once you make a big batch of this, weeknight meals go from boring to glorious. Serve it over chicken or with veggies and noodles, such as the Thai Noodles with Veggies (page 157). The ingredient list may look long but the sauce is simple to make and once it's done, you can make several meals from it.

4 garlic cloves, minced

2 tablespoons minced fresh ginger

2 teaspoons red pepper flakes

1½ cups creamy natural peanut butter, divided (salted is okay, but not sweetened)

1 tablespoon white shiro miso paste (see note)

3 tablespoons rice vinegar or cider vinegar

¼ cup soy sauce

2 tablespoons sesame oil

2 tablespoons honey

1 tablespoon freshly squeezed lime juice

¾ cup warm water, about 110°F

1. Place the garlic, ginger, red pepper flakes, and ¼ cup of the peanut butter, along with the miso paste, in a mortar and pestle or a small bowl. Grind well to combine the flavors. Transfer to a larger bowl and mix in the rest of the ingredients. Stir well to combine.

TO FREEZE: Use the Ice Cube Method (see page 16) to freeze. The easiest way is to use a silicone muffin pan, portioning out ½ cup of sauce into each muffin mold.

TO SERVE: Combine ½ cup of the peanut sauce with 1 cup of coconut milk.

NOTE: You can find miso paste in any Asian food market or most health food stores. This paste can also be used in salad dressings and stir-fries, and I've even heard of people using it in ice cream and brownies. Because it is a fermented food, it keeps well in the fridge.

Slow-Roasted Tomatoes

Yields 3 cups

Slow-roasted tomatoes should be stocked in everyone's kitchen. They intensify the flavor of just about anything. Throw them in soup, with hot pasta, on pizza, in quiche, or any other savory dish—the sky's the limit. They're also great chopped up in scrambled eggs in the morning.

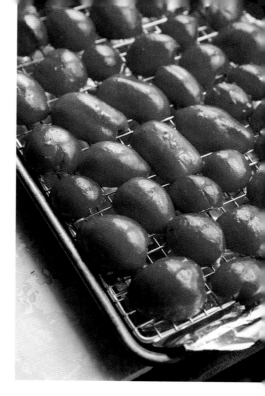

3 pounds tomatoes, Roma or smaller (firm tomatoes work best)

1 tablespoon olive oil

1 tablespoon sugar

1 teaspoon salt

½ teaspoon freshly ground black pepper

½ teaspoon dried thyme

1. Peeling the tomatoes is optional for slow-roasted tomatoes; oftentimes I skip this step, though I always peel for tomato sauce. If you desire to peel the tomatoes before roasting, refer to the directions in the Classic Tomato Sauce recipe (page 200).

2. Use a paring knife to remove the core from the top of the tomato. Slice the cored tomatoes in half. Use a small spoon to remove any seeds and juice, and reserve the juice for tomato sauce or tomato soup. If you're using a larger tomato, such as a Roma, quarter the tomatoes, but if the tomatoes are smaller, you can keep them in half. Toss the tomatoes with the oil, sugar, and seasonings.

3. Preheat the oven to 200°F. Line a half sheet pan with foil. Place a wire rack on top of the sheet pan. Lay the seasoned tomatoes, skin or exterior side up, on the rack. Roast for 5 to 7 hours, checking after 4 and 5 hours for doneness. The size of your tomatoes will cause the length of roasting to vary.

TO FREEZE: *Use the Divide and Portion Method (see page 15) to freeze. Vacuum-sealing works best for these, but if you don't have access to a vacuum sealer, store in pint-size freezer-safe resealable plastic bags. I've found ¼-cup portions are a good size.*

Chimichurri

Makes about 3 cups

My friend Kaleb made this for a very special dinner we shared with new friends. When he makes this chimichurri, he'll add some thinly sliced asparagus stalks along with a few asparagus heads, making the sauce a bit more vegetal and interesting. What's so great about this dish is how it can brighten up proteins such as steak or baked fish. We especially love it over Pork Tacos (page 123).

1 bunch of cilantro, finely chopped (about 1 cup)

1 bunch of parsley, finely chopped (about 1 cup)

Zest and juice of 2 lemons

Zest and juice of 2 limes

2 red jalapeño peppers, finely diced

1 small garlic bulb (8 to 10 cloves), minced

2 cups olive oil

2 teaspoons salt

¼ teaspoon freshly ground black pepper

1. Place all the ingredients in a medium-size bowl and stir to combine. I prefer some texture to this sauce, so I don't blend it, but you can also pulse it in a food processor for a smoother sauce. Taste and adjust the seasoning as needed. Serve over tacos, steak, or baked fish.

TO FREEZE: Use the Divide and Portion Method (page 15) to freeze.

Quick and Easy Enchilada Sauce

Makes 5 cups sauce

Homemade enchilada sauce is a great thing to have around, and not just for enchiladas. Use it to spice up eggs in Breakfast Burritos (page 67), over Mexican Rice and Black Bean bowls (page 74), or for the Sweet Potato Black Bean Burritos (page 124). Adjust the seasonings to your preference; that's the glory of making it at home!

2 tablespoons olive oil

2 medium yellow onions, diced

3 garlic cloves, minced

3 tablespoons chili powder

2 teaspoons ground cumin

1 tablespoon dark brown sugar

1 (28-ounce) can whole peeled tomatoes

½ cup Chicken Stock (page 202)

1 teaspoon salt

1. Heat a large saucepan over medium heat. Heat the oil, then add the onions and garlic. Sauté until the onions are soft and translucent, 2 to 3 minutes. Add the chili powder, cumin, and brown sugar and cook until fragrant. Add the tomatoes and stock, stirring with a wooden spoon to scrape up anything stuck to the bottom of the pan (the browned bits on the bottom enhance the flavor of any dish). Add the salt and simmer everything together for 5 minutes. Blend with an immersion blender or let cool, then blend using a high-powered blender.

TO FREEZE: Use the Divide and Portion Method (see page 15) to freeze. You may want to make a bag of 2 to 3 cups (for enchiladas) and then also a few bags of ½ cup or less for seasoning other foods, such as burritos.

Orange Sesame Stir-Fry Sauce

Makes enough sauce for 4 stir-fry recipes serving 4 each

As I was writing this book and making a stir-fry with frozen veggies, a lightbulb went off that I was missing a sauce . . . stir-fry sauce! While stir-fries are easy weeknight meals, making the sauce ahead of time makes them even easier.

---

2 cups freshly squeezed orange juice

1 cup soy sauce

1 cup vegetable stock

¼ cup sesame oil

¼ cup cornstarch

---

1. Place all the ingredients in a medium-size bowl. Use a whisk to combine well, then immediately divide into freezer bags before the mixture separates.

TO FREEZE: *Use the Divide and Portion Method (see page 15) to freeze. I use four pint-size freezer-safe resealable plastic bags filled with 1 cup of sauce in each bag for portions ready for stir-fries serving four people each.*

Pizza Dough

Makes enough dough for 2 pizzas

Making homemade pizza is way easier than you think it would be. Oftentimes it's messy but the mess is pretty much the only thing that requires effort, especially if you already have pizza dough on hand. When I make this recipe, I make two batches, freezing four dough balls total. The dough can be thawed in the fridge overnight and then used for calzones, pizza, or flatbread. Thanks to my friend Tyler for his genius pizza dough recipe.

---

1 (2¼-teaspoon) packet active dry yeast

1 teaspoon sugar

2 teaspoons kosher salt

4 cups bread flour (see note), plus more if needed

1½ cups warm water (110°F), plus more if needed

2 tablespoons olive oil

---

1. In a stand mixer with the dough hook attached, combine the yeast, sugar, salt, and bread flour. While the dry ingredients are still mixing, add the water, then the olive oil. This will form a large dough ball. If the dough is sticky, you may need to add more flour, 1 tablespoon at a time. If it is too dry, you can add more water, 1 tablespoon at a time. Once a solid dough ball is formed, move it onto floured surface and hand knead four or five folds, forming the dough into a ball shape.

2. Transfer the dough to a slightly oiled bowl, cover with plastic wrap or a moist towel, and place in a warm area of your kitchen to let rise for at least 1 hour. Once the dough has doubled in size, punch it down and separate into two equal-size balls Each ball will form a 14-inch or so pizza. You can use both balls at that time to make two pizzas, or use one and freeze the other for later use. Or freeze both!

TO FREEZE: Use the Wrap and Bag Method (page 16) to freeze. The dough will last 3 months in the freezer. To thaw, place in the fridge the night before you plan on using it. Remove from the fridge 2 hours before baking, placing the dough in a large oiled bowl covered with a slightly wet towel.
You can also roll out the dough and prepare it with toppings, then freeze the whole unbaked pizza (see page 16).

NOTE: Bread flour is key for crispier crust; you can substitute all-purpose flour for a chewier crust.

Sweet Potato Gnocchi

Makes about 6 cups gnocchi

My son helps me make gnocchi. He loves rolling the dough into balls and forming misshaped gnocchi. While he oftentimes turns his nose up at regular russet potato gnocchi, with sweet potato gnocchi his stomach knows no end. Plan on a few hours to make homemade sweet potato gnocchi and if you have some extra hands to help, double the recipe for a good freezer supply. Once it's made and frozen, you can add them into soups as little dumplings, or enjoy with some veggies and a tasty sauce.

2 pounds sweet potatoes
  (2 to 3 potatoes)
2 to 2½ cups all-purpose flour,
  plus more as needed

¼ cup grated Parmesan cheese
1½ teaspoons salt
1 large egg
2 teaspoons olive oil

1. Preheat the oven to 400°F. Prick the sweet potatoes with a fork and lay out on a foil-covered baking sheet. Bake for 30 minutes, then lower the heat to 350°F and bake for an additional 55 to 60 minutes, or until the potatoes are soft. Let potatoes cool just long enough to where you can handle them (you still want them pretty hot as you start the dough process). Then, use a potato ricer or a cheese grater (if you don't have a ricer) to rice the potatoes.

2. Place the riced potatoes in a large bowl (the biggest that you have) and add 2 cups of flour to start. Use your hands to toss the flour with the riced potatoes. If the mixture still seems too sticky, add up to ½ cup more flour. Add the cheese and salt. Make a well in the center and add the egg. The egg should help the dough come together into a ball. Add more flour, if needed.

3. Set out two rimmed baking sheets covered in parchment paper. Turn out the dough onto a floured surface and knead. Keep a small bowl of extra flour beside you as you work, adding more if the dough ball is sticky. Knead just enough to know that the mixture has enough flour to work with and the dough isn't sticky (over-kneading will result in tough gnocchi). Divide the dough into 12 to 14 equal-size balls. Roll out one ball at a time into a ½-inch-thick rope 9 to 10 inches long, flouring the rope as you go. Slice the rope into ½-inch squares or at an

angle for diamonds. Sometimes I like to cut into diamonds and skip the step of pressing with a fork, which also gives a nice presentation. For a traditional form, sprinkle the squares lightly with flour, then press the tines on the back of a fork into each small square, making an indentation of four lines.

4. Transfer the squares or diamonds to the parchment-lined baking sheets. Repeat with the remaining dough. This makes about two baking sheets of gnocchi, so plan on a good 30 to 45 minutes of rolling out the dough or bring in extra hands to help.

5. To cook, prepare a large, salted bowl of ice water for gnocchi and a few parchment- or tea towel–lined baking sheets. Bring a large pot of salted water to a boil. Add the gnocchi (one baking sheet's worth at a time). Boil for about 1 minute if you're freezing the gnocchi, or until they just begin to float to the top of the pot if you're planning to eat them that day (you're only partially cooking the ones you're freezing). Transfer the cooked gnocchi to the ice-water to stop the cooking. Only keep them in the ice water for a minute or two, tops, then transfer to the same parchment-lined baking sheets to dry and drain. Once the gnocchi are pretty dry, place them in a large bowl and toss lightly with the olive oil. Prepare the same baking sheets for freezing the gnocchi by wiping them down and laying out two fresh parchment sheets.

TO FREEZE: Use the Lay Out and Freeze Method (see page 14) to freeze the oiled gnocchi.

NOTE: You may use russet potatoes in this recipe for traditional gnocchi. Follow the same directions. Sweet potato gnocchi sometimes require more flour because the potatoes are less dry when cooked.

Pasta Dough

This is a basic dough that you can use for any type of pasta. It works well with a pasta machine, too. In this book we use it for ravioli but you could also use it to make homemade spaghetti for the Shrimp and Zucchini Spaghetti on page 162.

2 cups all-purpose flour, plus more for dusting

1 teaspoon salt

3 large eggs

2 teaspoons cold water

2 teaspoons olive oil

1. In a stand mixer fitted with the dough hook attachment, mix together the flour and salt. Add the eggs, one at a time. Between the egg additions, use a spatula to push down any excess flour off the mixer and into the dough. Add the water and oil, then let the mixer knead the dough until a ball starts to form.

2. Turn out the dough onto a floured work surface along with any scraps and extra flour from the mixing bowl. To knead, use your fingers and the palm of your hand to fold the dough over and push it out. Knead the dough until it is elastic with a sheen on the outside, 5 to 10 minutes.

3. Wrap the finished dough in plastic wrap, then let it rest for 20 to 30 minutes on the counter or overnight in the fridge.

4. Divide the dough into four portions. Roll out each portion of dough, using a pasta machine, according to the manufacturer's directions for the cut of pasta you're making.

Ravioli

Makes about 40 ravioli

These are the basic directions to make any homemade ravioli. For this book, we're using the Butternut Squash Filling on page 151. If you choose to use another filling, just make sure that it does not have any excess liquid.

All-purpose flour, for dusting
1 recipe Pasta Dough, page 218
 (see note)

1 large egg, whisked, for sealing
 the dough

---

1. Dust a large or long work surface with flour. Line two baking sheets with parchment paper and set out the whisked egg in a small bowl near your work surface. Divide the rested pasta dough ball into four segments. Use a pasta machine or a stand mixer pasta attachment to roll out the dough. Start with the number 1 setting, moving through one of the segments of the dough. Go through each setting though the number 6, passing the dough through the roller and brushing it with flour between each setting. Repeat with the remaining pasta segments. Lay out the strips on the prepared work surface.

2. Use a ravioli cutter or a sharp knife to cut the dough into 1½- to 2-inch squares. If using a ravioli cutter, make sure to press down hard to fully cut through the pasta. Place a heaping teaspoon of filling on every other square. Use a pastry brush or your fingers to brush the egg wash onto the edges of the ravioli. Lay an empty square on top of a filled one and seal, using the side of your finger. Continue until all the ravioli are assembled.

3. **To cook:** Bring a large pot of salted water to a boil. Carefully drop in the prepared ravioli and cook in boiling water until they rise to the surface. Remove with a slotted spoon to a serving dish and top with prepared sauce. Serve immediately.

4. **To freeze:** Use the Lay Out and Freeze Method (see page 14) to freeze assembled, uncooked ravioli.

NOTE: Homemade pasta for ravioli can be replaced by wonton wrappers for an easy and quick alternative to making your own pasta at home.

ACKNOWLEDGMENTS

Many friends helped me with this book along the way. Though I had many ideas for the topic of freezing, like I said before, I was no expert at freezing and didn't even regularly practice freezing until I started this book. My chef friend Adam opened up his freezer to me and gave me lots of tips and secrets, as well as my friend Anne—who I'll just call the freezer extraordinaire—who showed me her wildly organized freezer. Inspiration was also found through my culinary education at Park City Culinary Institute with chefs Mary Check, Houman Gohary, and Adam Kreisel. My friends Haley, Annalise, Lindsey, and Becky, who are fellow bloggers and dear friends, helped here and there with this book—maybe even unknowingly! As a self-aware bad speller, I am grateful for Levi and Heidi who helped me edit my sometimes sloppy thoughts. I have so much gratitude for all of my friends who supported me along the way through babysitting, eating and preparing freezer meals, and letting me rant about my new excitement for freezing foods—thank you Sandy, Heather, Alexis, Heidi, and Bekah. And last but of course not least, I wouldn't be successful at much without the help and love of my husband Josh, who edited countless photos, created graphs, and also wrote my bio. Clearly, it takes a whole village for me!

If you would like more information on the topic of freezing, please refer to the Food Safety and Inspection Service USDA website. You may also find the following resources helpful: *Canning and Preserving for Dummies*, Amelia Jeanroy (Wiley For Dummies, 2009) and StillTasty.com.

INDEX